PRINCE OF PREACHERS

The Apostle Paul

Paul Gericke

University Press of America,® Inc.
Lanham · Boulder · New York · Toronto · Oxford

Copyright © 2006 by
University Press of America,® Inc.
4501 Forbes Boulevard
Suite 200
Lanham, Maryland 20706
UPA Acquisitions Department (301) 459-3366

PO Box 317
Oxford
OX2 9RU, UK

All rights reserved
Printed in the United States of America
British Library Cataloging in Publication Information Available

Library of Congress Control Number: 2005937940
ISBN 978-0-7618-3391-8

"Scripture taken from the HOLY BIBLE, NEW
INTERNATIONAL VERSION. Copyright © 1973, 1978, 1984
International Bible Society. Used by permission of Zondervan
Bible Publishers."
Some editions of the NIV texts vary slightly,
but the meaning is essentially the same.

∞™ The paper used in this publication meets the minimum
requirements of American National Standard for Information
Sciences—Permanence of Paper for Printed Library Materials,
ANSI Z39.48—1984

DEDICATION

To all the people that
the Lord has called to
proclaim the word of God

CONTENTS

ACKNOWLEDGMENTS

INTRODUCTION 1
   I. HIS LIFE 3
   II. HIS CHARACTER 9
   III. HIS MESSAGES 17
   IV. HIS DOCTRINE 29
   V. HIS ORGANIZATION OF MESSAGES 37
   VI. HIS STYLE OF SPEAKING 43
   VII. HIS POWER AND EFFECTIVENESS 49
   VIII. HIS INSTRUCTIONS ON PREACHING 55

SUMMARY 73

CONCLUSION 79

REFERENCES 81

BIOGRAPHICAL SKETCH 83

ACKNOWLEDGMENTS

I am grateful to Zondervan Bible Publishers for permission to quote Scripture from the Holy Bible, New International Version, published by the International Bible Society. Without this significant source the book could not have been written and published.

Thanks to the University Press of America and the staff who were helpful in the preparation and the publication of the book, particularly David Choa in getting the preparation of the book started and Beverly Baum in arranging the material.

I am indebted to Bruce Ayscue, a teacher of English, for his time and diligence in proofreading and editing my manuscript.

Thanks also to my devoted neighbor and fellow Christian H. Mack Anders for his time and computer expertise in reviewing and formatting my manuscript for publication.

INTRODUCTION

Since Jesus Christ is the Lord of Preachers, the greatest of his servants is the Apostle Paul, who is Prince of Preachers. Much has been written about his life, his ministry, his theology, his ethics, and his letters, but little has been written about one of his greatest gifts, preaching. When Paul refers to his calling, he first lists preaching, then apostleship and teaching (I Timothy 2:7 and II Timothy 1:11).

A few books have been written on the preaching of the Apostle Paul in the last two centuries from John Eadie in 1860 to Raymond Bailey in 1991 and several dissertations including those written by Charles Chamberlain in 1959 and Donald Sunukjian in 1972. Most of these do not deal with the preaching of Paul generally and specifically as an art, but some phase of it or application of his ministry. Since Paul considered preaching as primary in his many-sided calling and ministry, a thorough discussion of this matter is appropriate. Paul spent much of his ministry preaching the gospel throughout the Roman world with great effectiveness, and he had much to say about preaching in letters to the churches and to ministers about this important ministry. Much can be learned that can be of help and encouragement to ministers, lay preachers, and churches today (See References).

The purpose of this book, therefore, is to study the preaching of the Apostle Paul and his writings on this matter to discover the message, principles, and methods of preaching manifested in his life, ministry, and writings. The hope is that those who preach, teach, and proclaim the word of God will discover the ways this prince of preachers was so effective in this strategic ministry and seek to manifest these principles of preaching in their ministries.

The primary source of the study is the New Testament, namely the book of Acts and the letters of the Apostle Paul. However, some secondary sources are used, although not cited, such as those mentioned above and chapters in some books on the life, ministry, and teachings of Paul.

The approach of the study is to describe the preaching of Paul by an exposition of the various passages in the New Testament that report his messages and by an exegesis of key words and expressions used for preaching or some aspect of preaching and by passages that explain its use or importance.

First of all, Paul's life, personality, and ministry are studied in order to provide the proper background for the study of his preaching. His sermons are analyzed followed by a presentation of his major doctrines and ethical views. His sermon structure, elements, and style are studied and are followed by an analysis of the effects and the power of his preaching. In the light of his preaching and its effectiveness, his instructions on preaching are discussed. A summary with a conclusion is offered evaluating his preaching, noting reasons for its effectiveness and its contributions to his own ministry and to preaching today. With his example in mind, a plea for New Testament preaching is offered to those who proclaim the word of God.

CHAPTER I

HIS LIFE

The Apostle Paul is first mentioned in the book of Acts of the New Testament by his given name Saul, a young man approving the death of Stephen. He was a Jew of the Dispersion, born in the Gentile city of Tarsus at the foot of the Cilician hills in what is known today as Turkey. The city was strategically located on the crossroads between east and west by land and by sea, a port city on the Mediterranean. It was controlled by the Roman government, but influenced by Greek culture. Its citizens had Roman citizenship. Greek apparently was the native language there, since Saul quoted from the Greek Septuagint, a translation of the Hebrew Old Testament, but Aramaic was his secondary language, a language closely related to Hebrew.

With his inheritance of the Greek culture and language, Saul was able to communicate with most of the known world at that time, which was necessary to reach the world for Christ. However, his basic beliefs were Hebrew in origin. He was the son of a Pharisee, the strict party of the Jews, with a Hellenistic Jewish family background. He studied under Gamaliel in Jerusalem and was a diligent student of this renown teacher of the Pharisaic party. He was patriotic and zealous with a strong personal pride and ambition. He was marked by keen analytical thought and with depth of moral and religious conviction. He was capable of acute argumentation and rhetorical skill in his disputations at Antioch, Athens, and Ephesus. But he was a Hebrew of Hebrews, a devout Jew of the Dispersion, but a citizen of the Roman Empire.

His Conversion to Christ

Saul of Tarsus, debtor to both Jews and Greeks, no doubt had been to Jerusalem a number of times during Jewish festivals and his studies under Gamaliel. He could have been there during Jesus' public ministry. He would have been a young man at the time, taking part in his studies and in meetings of the Pharisees. He appeared to be schooled for the Sanhedrin, the ruling body of the Jews. He certainly became aware eventually of the rejection and crucifixion of Jesus by the Jews and the Romans and the story of the establishment of the primitive church.

During the stoning of Stephen, the first Christian martyr, Saul was passively consenting to his death. This experience no doubt made a deep impression on him, convicting his heart and mind on the one hand, but also stirring up a hostility that led to the persecution of the early church. He had men and women dragged off to prison, breathing threats of murder against the disciples. He gained approval from the high priests and received letters to the synagogues of Damascus to bring the followers of the way as prisoners to Jerusalem (Acts 8:1-3; 9:1-2).

On his way to Damascus, a light from heaven flashed around him, and he fell to the ground and heard a voice saying, "Saul, Saul, why do you persecute me?" When he asked, "Who are you, Lord?" He replied, "I am Jesus, whom you are persecuting." He was told to get up and go into the city where he would be told what he must do. Saul got up but could not see. This recognition of Jesus as Lord indicated that he had committed his life to Christ, a turning point in history (Acts 9:3-8). The men traveling with him heard the sound, but saw no one. They led him to Damascus, and for three days he was blind and did not eat or drink. In the mean time the Lord instructed and persuaded a man named Ananias to go to the house of Judas on the street called Straight where Saul was praying. Ananias was reluctant to go because of the report that he was persecuting Christians in Jerusalem (Acts 9:10-16).

His Commission

But then the Lord convinced Ananias, saying, "Go! This man is my choice instrument to carry my name before the Gentiles and their kings and before the people Israel. I will show him how much he must suffer for my name" (Acts 9:15-16). He went to the house and placed his hands on Saul and said, "Brother Saul, the Lord—Jesus, who appeared to you on the road as you were coming here—has sent me so that you may see again and be filled with the Holy Spirit" (Acts 9:17). Immediately something like scales fell from his eyes and he could see. He arose and was baptized, and he gained strength when he took some food. In his testimony before the Jews in Jerusalem later, he gave this view of Ananias' message, "The God of our fathers has chosen you to know his will and to see the Righteous One and to hear words from his mouth. You will be his witness to all men of what you have seen and heard" (Acts 22:14-15).

After several days in Damascus, Saul, filled with the Spirit, began to preach in the synagogues that Jesus is the Son of God. All who heard him were astonished saying, "Isn't he the man who raised havoc in Jerusalem among those who called on his name? And hasn't he come here to take them as prisoners to the chief priests?" (Acts 9:21). The Jews then conspired to kill him, but he escaped when his followers lowered him in a basket through an opening in the city wall. Some time later he spent three years in Arabia for meditation and reassessment of his views on theology in the light of his conversion and of the life, death, and resurrection of Christ. In Jerusalem he was hated by the Jews as a traitor, and Christ's followers held him with suspicion. But Barnabas stood with him and won an opportunity to allow him to appear before the apostles, telling them how the Lord Jesus appeared to him on the road to Damascus and how he preached boldly that Jesus is the Christ. Henceforth, Paul moved about in Jerusalem, speaking boldly in the name of the Lord and debating with Grecian Jews. When they sought to kill him, the disciples sent him off to Caesarea and then off to Tarsus. The church, strengthened and encouraged by the Holy Spirit, grew in numbers (Acts 9:23-31).

Saul spent several years in his home city Tarsus and also in nearby areas preaching the word of God. After some time Barnabas came from Antioch and found him to help with the work among the Gentiles, who were turning to the Lord in Antioch and the surrounding areas. A great number of people believed in the Lord, and these new disciples were first called Christians there (Acts 11:22-26).

His First Missionary Journey

Barnabas and Saul were among the prophets and teachers at Antioch. While they were worshiping the Lord and fasting, the Holy Spirit said, "Set apart for me Barnabas and Saul for the work to which I have called them." After they fasted and prayed, they placed their hands on them and sent them off (Acts 13:1-3). They left Antioch and sailed to Cyprus on their first missionary journey and then on to Asia Minor. Saul, who was then called Paul, preached the word of God in the Jewish synagogues with great power and effectiveness. This is exemplified by his message at Antioch of Pisidia. There he proclaimed the death and the resurrection of Jesus for the forgiveness of sins, justifying man from all that the Law of Moses could not do. A group of believers, called the church, was gathered in the various cities, and elders were appointed to lead the disciples. Many of the Jewish rabbis stirred up opposition and persecuted the Christians; so Paul and Barnabas turned to the Gentiles, many of whom received the word with gladness. They spread the word of the Lord through many trials and tribulations, and many Jews and Gentiles believed. When they returned to Antioch, they gathered the church and reported what God had done through them, opening the door of faith to the Gentiles (Acts 13:4-14:28). A group of Christians who were called Judaizers came from Jerusalem to Antioch claiming that Gentiles needed to keep the Mosaic laws in order to become Christians. They were challenged along with other leaders regarding this critical issue of the early church. Later at the first conference of the church called in Jerusalem, Peter, John, and James, the Lord's half brother, concurred with Paul and Barnabas that Gentile Christians need not keep the Jewish laws, including circumcision, to become Christians. Salvation comes by grace through faith alone, not by including works. They sent a circular letter stating this fact, but requested that Gentiles abstain from food offered to idols, from blood, from meat of strangled animals, and from sexual immorality. There was great rejoicing among the Gentile Christians over hearing the equality of believers, who are saved by the grace of Christ alone (Acts 15:1-35).

His Second Missionary Journey

After some time had passed, Paul asked Barnabas to accompany him on a second missionary journey to Asia Minor to preach the word and to see how the churches were progressing. But in a disagreement over taking Mark with them, who abandoned them on the first trip, Barnabas took him to Cyprus. Paul chose Silas and was commended by the disciples to the grace of the Lord. Traveling through Syria and Cilicia, they strengthened the churches there, and they established new churches. They enlisted Timothy at Lystra to join them on their journey. They were forbidden by the Holy Spirit to travel southwest in the province of Asia Minor and also not allowed to enter Bithynia to the north, so they traveled west on the Roman roads to Troas. Here they were joined by Luke the physician, the writer of the Gospel of Luke and Acts (Acts 15:36-16:8). At that time Paul saw a vision of a man from Macedonia begging him to come and help them. Paul concluded that God had called them to preach the gospel there, a decision of great consequences for world missions. The first convert was Lydia, a woman of means, at a prayer meeting on the Sabbath by the river outside of the city gates of Philippi. She opened her heart to the Lord with her household, and they were baptized. The disciples remained with her for a period of time and began to evangelize the Roman colony (Acts 16:11-15).

While preaching around Philippi, Paul was filled with the Spirit, but a slave girl with a spirit of fortune-telling followed him, telling the people that they were servants of God showing the way to be saved. This became annoying to Paul, and he cast out the spirit. When the exploiters of the girl lost their business because of this, they convinced the magistrates to have them beaten and thrown into prison. During an earthquake which shook the prison foundation and opened the prison doors, Paul led the fearful jailer to Christ, who asked, "Sirs, what must I do to be saved?" He replied, "Believe in the Lord Jesus, and you will be saved—you and your household." They spoke the word of the Lord to him and his whole household. They rejoiced in believing in God and helped Paul and Silas to recover from their beating. An active church was established in Philippi in the days that they were there (Acts 16:16-40).

Traveling onward into Macedonia, Paul and Silas preached the word and led many to Christ in Thessalonica and Berea, but aroused opposition from the Jews. They continued on to Athens where Paul was stirred in his heart by the idolatry there, and testified to the Greeks in the agora and the Acropolis with minimal success. He then spent two years in Corinth where he had a great ingathering of people to Christ and established a number of churches with gifted leaders. The Jews, however, again opposed him, but the proconsul refused to condemn Paul and in fact gave Christians a place as a sect of Judaism before Roman law. Paul wrote two letters to the Thessalonians, including matters concerning the second coming of Christ. He left Corinth with fellow believers Aquila and Priscilla for Ephesus, and leaving them there, he made a trip back to Antioch via Caesarea (Acts 18:18-22).

His Third Missionary Journey

After sending some time there, he embarked on his third missionary journey through Galatia and Phrygia, strengthening all the disciples. He then went on to Ephesus. He lived and served there with unusual effectiveness for three years, evangelizing the western section of Asia Minor and performing many miracles.

There was opposition including a riot by the followers of the goddess Diana. However, many people were responding to Paul's preaching. He wrote several letters to the church at Corinth, including instructions regarding truths of the word of God and corrections regarding misunderstandings and abuses. He wrote other letters to the Galatians and the Romans presenting the gospel in its fullness. He defended justification by grace through faith in the work of Christ on the cross for both Jews and Gentiles. Paul planned to return to Jerusalem with a collection for the poor saints there and then travel to Rome and Spain. He went to Philippi and preached along the way with Luke as his associate. He met with the elders of the church of Ephesus at the coastal city of Miletus on his return to Jerusalem by the way of Tyre and Caesarea, being warned by the Lord of dangers ahead (Acts 19:23-20:38).

In Jerusalem the Judaizers were stirring up hostility, claiming Paul was telling Jewish Christians not to keep the ceremonial law. But he was well received by James and other Christian leaders. Paul was seen offering vows and keeping purification rites during the Feast of Pentecost trying to silence criticism, but the Judaizers claimed he was desecrating the temple by bringing Greeks into the temple court. A mob gathered and dragged Paul out of the temple and was about to kill him, but he was rescued by the soldiers of the Roman governor. On the steps of the Tower of Antonia, Paul was given permission to speak in his defense, but when he said that he was sent to preach to the Gentiles, the Jews raised a furious commotion. The Roman commander was ready to flog him to find out the problem, but Paul told him that he was a Roman citizen. So he was sent before the Sanhedrin to resolve the conflict. In the debate Paul set the Pharisees against the Sadducees regarding the resurrection from the dead. When a plot was discovered to kill him, he was sent then to Caesarea. He appeared in a trial before governor Felix, who delayed his decision regarding the charges, hoping to receive a bribe from him (Acts 21:17-24:26).

But after two years Felix was succeeded by governor Festus. Paul had appealed to Caesar in hope for justice. He appeared before Festus, King Agrippa II, and leaders of the court to defend himself, but to no avail. They found nothing that deserved death, but since he appealed to Caesar, he was sent to Rome (Acts 25:1-26:32).

His Fourth Missionary Journey

The last missionary journey of Paul was his voyage to Rome at the expense of the Romans. Under the command of the centurion Julius and a group of soldiers, Paul with other prisoners was shipped to Rome. They met with disaster and were shipwrecked on the island of Malta. All the cargo was lost, but all the people were saved by God's mercy through Paul's prayers and divine guidance (Acts 27:1-44). The winter was spent there, but in the spring the passengers found a grain ship bound for Rome. Paul was met on the way at Puteoli by brethren alerted from Rome and went with them into the city. He found some favor with the Jews who had heard of his problems in Jerusalem. He was kept under house arrest for two years, but had access to Christians who visited him often. Luke ended his record of Paul's life there, but gathered information needed to complete his writing of the book of Acts (Acts 28:1-31).

Paul needed about five years to defend himself. He was able to win to Christ a few of the soldiers chained to him and some visitors to him in his hired house. Timothy and Luke were with him often to help spread the gospel. He wrote letters to the Philippian and Colossian churches regarding truth and life and the errors of the Gnostics about Christ and the Christian life. Other circular letters were written to the Ephesians and the Laodiceans and his appeal to Philemon on behalf of Onesimus, the converted runaway slave. Paul was probably freed from prison and left Rome for two years. When Nero set fire to the city of Rome, charging Christians for the disaster, the situation made it a criminal offence to be a Christian.

During this time Paul had traveled to Macedonia where he wrote his first letter to Timothy. He probably traveled west to Spain later, but was arrested back in Rome and placed in a dungeon. Only Luke was with him to the end, but he wrote a letter to Titus and a second letter to Timothy which was his last recorded letter, his swan song. We know nothing of his death, which probably occurred before the summer of A.D. 68, the year of Emperor Nero's death, when persecution and death were extensive. So this ended the remarkable life of this dedicated Minster of Christ: preacher, apostle, and teacher of the Gentiles.

Paul fulfilled his calling to proclaim Jesus Christ, the Son of God and Savior, from his experience with the Lord on the road to Damascus to the very end of his life. In the book of Acts, Luke recorded the beginning of Paul's life and ministry, preaching Jesus the Son of God boldly and without hindrance until the end of his record of preaching the kingdom of God and teaching about the Lord Jesus Christ (Acts 28:23-31). During his ministry of about thirty-five years, he preached the word of God in much of the civilized world as a missionary, he developed and clarified the foundational truths of Scripture, and he manifested the courage fitting of Christians, especially ministers of the gospel. He wrote letters that became part of the canon of the New Testament and left a legacy of life and service for Luke to record in the Acts of the Apostles. All that he accomplished was not through his own ability, but through the Lord Jesus Christ who enabled him (Philippians 4:13).

CHAPTER II

HIS CHARACTER

What was the character of Saul of Tarsus before his conversion? What were his natural abilities? Since he was raised in a Roman-controlled city of Asia Minor, he was no doubt influenced by both Greek and Roman culture. However, he was a thoroughgoing Jew of the sect of the Pharisees and influenced by his devout parents and the local synagogue and school. Saul had a passion for the Jewish faith and morality, which preoccupied his life and reinforced his pride and ability to succeed. He received a wealth of knowledge from the Old Testament; the Pentateuch, the prophets, and psalms permeated all that he said and did. After his conversion, they became a source of authority, but interpreted by the Spirit of God, along with his New Testament revelations.

Paul matured early in character in his Christian life. From the Greek world and culture, especially the Greek language, he developed an analytical mind with an argumentative style. He also seemed influenced by stoicism manifested in his use of rhetorical questions from imaginary objectors including argumentation, which also gave him a rhetorical style. But in spite of the Greek and Roman influence, he manifested a strong religious and moral nature, though sometimes misguided before he was saved, leading him to dogmatic and dangerous conclusions and actions. This led to his persecution of the early church and its teachings, which he thought were contrary to the true faith of the Jews.

Love of Christ

The love of Christ was the dominating influence in the life of Paul. He wrote to the Corinthians: "For Christ's love compels us, because we are convinced that one died for all, and therefore all died. And he died for all, that those who live should no longer live for themselves but for him who died for them and was raised again" (2 Corinthians 5:14-15).

Christ's love motivated him and compelled him to serve faithfully. In his great love chapter in 1 Corinthians 13, he wrote that this most important gift was far superior to such gifts as all the languages, prophecies, mysteries, and knowledge that the Christian may have or manifest. He described love's characteristics as being patient and kind, not self-seeking or rude, but protecting and giving hope with all perseverance. The greatest gifts are faith, hope, and love, but the greatest is love. He believed this and lived this out in his Christian life (1 Corinthians 13:1-13).

Furthermore, Paul was convinced that "in all things God works for the good of those who love him, who have been called according to his purpose" (Romans 8:28). Moreover, he believed that nothing could separate him from the love of Christ (Romans 8:38-39). Through all his struggles, hardships, and persecutions, he lived for Christ whom he loved because he first loved him. For Christ would always be present to help him in whatever circumstances and problems that he would encounter.

Dedication to Christ

In his letter to the Romans, Paul described in the first part of the letter God's great salvation plan of his love and mercy for everyone (Romans 1-11). He then appealed to the Christian to make a decisive dedication of his life to Christ as a reasonable service. He declared, "Therefore, I urge you, brothers, in view of God's mercy, to offer your bodies as living sacrifices, holy and pleasing to God—this is your spiritual act of worship" (Romans 12:1). He described this decision earlier in the letter in which he included an appeal to make a once for all offer of life with all parts of the body to Christ (Romans 6:13). In both passages he used the aorist tense, which indicates point action, that is, a decisive dedication or once-for-all offer. In both passages he also used the imperative mood indicating a command. This decision gave him the personal victory in his early struggles of his life as described in the seventh chapter of Romans. In verse fourteen he shifted to the present tense indicating that he had a spiritual battle as a Christian. He wrote, "For what I do is not the good I want to do; no, the evil I do not want to do—this I keep on doing....it is sin living in me that does it" (Romans 7:19-20). He cried out, "What a wretched man I am! Who will rescue me from this body of death? Thanks be to God—through Jesus Christ our Lord!" (Romans 7:24-25). He described how he got the victory in the following chapter in Romans, which was by the Holy Spirit who set him free and gave him peace of heart and mind. He was delivered through the death of the old nature and through a new nature by the Spirit (Romans 8:1-17). Sometime in his early Christian life he made this decision for Christ before he embarked on his missionary journeys. He claimed, "We are more than conquerors through him who loved us" (Romans 8:37). Paul was wholly dedicated to Christ his Lord: body, soul, and spirit. This was manifested in his accomplishments in his ministry.

Determination

To the Corinthians Paul wrote, "For I resolved to know nothing while I was with you except Jesus Christ and him crucified" (1 Corinthians 2:2). He resolved to keep focused on Christ whose primary goal was to pay the sin debt of men and save them through faith. In this matter he manifested a strong will of determination. To the Philippians he wrote that he was forgetting what was behind him and pressing toward what was ahead, the goal to win the prize for which God had called him heavenward in Christ Jesus. Whatever was to his profit according to the flesh, he considered a loss for the sake of Christ. This included his Jewish heritage of the people of Israel and the tribe of Benjamin, his being a Hebrew of Hebrews, his zeal as a Pharisee, his persecution of the church, and his faultless life in righteousness according to the law. He considered all these as loss compared to knowing Christ and the power of his resurrection and the fellowship of his sufferings, becoming like him in his death and attaining the resurrection from the dead (Philippians 3:4-11). Thus he strove all his life as a Christian for these goals so that at the end of his life on earth he could tell Timothy in his second letter to him:

> I have fought the good fight, I have finished the race, I have kept the faith. Now there is in store for me the crown of righteousness, which the Lord, the righteous Judge, will award me on that day—and not only to me, but also to all who have longed for his appearing (2 Timothy 4:7-8).

Boldness

After Paul met the Lord on the road to Damascus and gave his life to Christ, he received his sight again, was baptized, and filled with the Holy Spirit. After taking some food, he regained his strength in a few days and began preaching in the synagogues that Jesus is the Son of God. As on the Day of Pentecost when the disciples were filled with the Spirit, he preached boldly and with great power, giving evidence of the power of the Spirit. He grew more and more powerful, proving that Jesus is the Christ, the Jewish Messiah, confounding the Jewish leaders.

When Barnabas took Paul before the apostles, he told them how the Lord had spoken to him and how he had preached fearlessly in the name of Jesus in Damascus. He stayed in Jerusalem and moved about freely for a time, speaking boldly in the name of the Lord (Acts 9:20-22). In his first letter to the Thessalonians, he wrote:

> For we know, brothers loved by God, that he has chosen you, because our gospel came to you not simply with words, but also with power, with the Holy Spirit and with deep conviction. You know how we lived among you for your sake. You became imitators of us and of the Lord; in spite of severe suffering, you welcomed the message with joy given by the Holy Spirit (1 Thessalonians 1:4-6).

Thus, he urged the Ephesians to be filled with the Spirit (Ephesians 5:18b). This was a command given to Christians to be continually filled with the Spirit. It is passive action, performed by the Spirit on all Christians who empty themselves of the things of the world and of selfish ambition and then pray and accept the power and boldness available to them. All Christians are sealed with the Spirit, but they need to be and can be empowered by him (Ephesians 1:13; 3:16; 5:18).

Righteousness

Out of Paul's background came his view of righteousness, which came by keeping the law of Moses, advocated by the strict interpretation of the law by the Pharisees. This righteousness was based on the Old Testament. However, when he met Christ and trusted him as Savior and Lord, he realized that God requires the righteousness that he provides through the gospel: the death, burial, and resurrection of Christ. He paid man's sin debt and provided his righteousness to those who believe in him. Thus, Paul was not ashamed of the gospel, but proclaimed it since it is the power of God unto salvation to everyone who believes. For in the gospel God's righteousness is revealed, a righteousness that comes through faith from first to last (Romans 1:17). He realized that this is what Habakkuk had prophesied, "The righteous will live by his faith" (Habakkuk 2:4).

Righteousness was the major theme of Paul's letter to the Romans. He began by stating, "For all have sinned and fall short of the glory of God" (Romans 3:23). Furthermore, "For the wages of sin is death, but the gift of God is eternal life in Christ Jesus our Lord" (Romans 6:23). He cited the experience of Abraham, the father of the faithful, who believed God, and it was credited to him as righteousness (Genesis 15:6 and Romans 4:3). Paul went on to explain that righteousness was credited to those who believed God raised Jesus our Lord from the dead to confirm that he was delivered unto death for our sins and raised to life for our justification (Romans 4:24-25). "God demonstrates his own love for us in this: While we were still sinners, Christ died for us" (Romans 5:8). Moses described the way of righteousness through the law, but by the law comes the knowledge of sin, not salvation. But God's righteousness is given to those who believe. Thus, believers are credited with righteousness according to their standing before God and receive righteousness to live in this present world.

The message that Paul proclaimed is that righteousness comes through faith. He wrote in his letter to the Romans:

> That if you confess with your mouth, 'Jesus is Lord,' and believe in your heart that God raised him from the dead, you will be saved. For it is with your heart that you believe and are justified, and it is with your mouth that you confess and are saved (Romans 10:9-10).

Anyone trusting in Christ can live the Christian life daily, since he is enabled, through the grace that God gives him (Romans 6:17-19). This Paul believed and put into practice in his daily living. What Christ lived and proclaimed, Paul manifested in his life by the Spirit of Christ.

Faith

Closely related to Paul's view of righteousness is his view of faith, as seen in his letter to the Romans and its origin in Scripture in Habakkuk's prophecy as noted above, "The righteous will live by his faith" (Habakkuk 2:4). Abraham is called the father of the faithful, and thus all believers become children of Abraham by faith. Paul cites this relationship between the righteous, or just, living by faith in Romans

1:17 and in Galatians 2:16 and 3:11. In his letter to the Galatians, he goes on to explain that Christ has redeemed us from the curse of the law in order that Gentiles might receive the promise of the Spirit (Galatians 3:13-14).

Furthermore, Paul stressed, "For it is by grace you have been saved, through faith—and this not from yourselves, it is the gift of God—not by works, so that no one can boast" (Ephesians 2:8-9). But he had a place for works, for he continued, "For we are God's workmanship, created in Christ Jesus to do good works, which God prepared in advance for us to do" (Ephesians 2:10). Thus, it is by grace that people are saved through faith, but believers are prepared by God to do good works that he ordains. Paul shows the relationship between faith and works, even as James wrote in his general letter that believers demonstrate true faith by the good works that they do (James 2:18-19; 22-24). The author of the letter to the Hebrews also cites Habakkuk, writing, "But my righteous one will live by faith" (Hebrews 10:38). He illustrates this by a long list of believers who acted on faith producing good works motivated by the Lord to his honor and glory (Hebrews 11:1-40). Paul could be added to this list, for he suffered for Christ's sake, looking forward with a great cloud of witnesses to a better world with his eyes on Jesus, the author and perfecter of his faith.

Vision

From the time of his conversion, Paul knew he was a chosen vessel. His calling was to carry the name of Christ to the Gentiles (Acts 9:15-16). He reminded Timothy in both his letters to him that he was called to be a preacher, an apostle, and a teacher of the faith to the Gentiles (1 Timothy 2:7; 2 Timothy 1:11). He knew that he had an obligation to both Greeks and Jews, to the wise and the foolish, and was eager to preach the gospel at Rome (Romans 1:14-15).

He began by preaching boldly to the people in Damascus, continued with the help of Barnabas in Jerusalem, then in Tarsus, and in Antioch, which became the base for his missionary journeys in Asia Minor and Europe. His journeys ended in Rome as recorded in Acts. He probably preached another two years, which included Spain and other parts Europe. His journeys were guided and directed by the Holy Spirit, as indicated in his journey through Asia Minor to Troas. There he received a vision of a man from Macedonia to come over and help them, and he concluded that God had called him to preach the gospel to these people. On these trips he preached the gospel first to the Jews, but when he was usually rejected by most of the leadership, he turned to the Gentiles who generally received him gladly. The Jews often stirred up opposition and persecuted the group of believers, but he remained steadfast to his calling.

So important was his ministry to world missions that his conversion, calling, and vision were recorded three times in the book of Acts, and over one-half of this book covers his ministry. His conversion and calling are recorded in the ninth chapter, and this testimony and his vision are recorded twice more, once before the

Jews in Jerusalem and then to the Gentiles and to the Jews in Caesarea (Acts 9:1-30; 21:33-22:21; 26:1-29). In each of these passages, his primary mission to the Gentiles is presented according to his vision and command given by the Lord.

Prayerfulness

Paul was a man of prayer, from his first recorded prayers, "Who are you, Lord?" and "What shall I do, Lord?" (Acts 9:5; 22:8-10), and to his last recorded prayer request in his final greeting in his second letter to Timothy, "The Lord be with your spirit. Grace be with you" (2 Timothy 4:22). He prayed prayers of praise, confession, petition, thanksgiving, and intercession, as he talked to the Lord and listened for the answers. To the Ephesians he recorded his prayer and thanksgiving for God's redemption through the blood of Christ, his forgiveness of sins according to his grace, and the inheritance given to the praise of his glory (Ephesians 1:3-23). He prayed for them to be strengthened through the Spirit and to be filled with all the fullness of God (Ephesians 3:14-21). He prayed a similar prayer of praise, thanksgiving, and intercession in his letter to the Colossians (Colossians 1:9-14). In his letter to the Romans, he described his appeal for the necessity of prayer in the confession of faith and for calling on the Lord to be saved (Romans 10:9-10, 13). He prayed for the lost people of Israel that they might be saved (Romans 10:1-4), and he indicated his heaviness of heart and sorrow for them even to the extent of being cursed and cut off from Christ (Romans 9:1-4). To Timothy he exhorted that requests, prayers, intercessions, and thanksgivings be made for all men to be saved and come to the knowledge of the truth (1 Timothy 2:1-4). He appealed for prayers for all in authority that Christians might lead a quiet and peaceful life in all godliness and holiness (1 Timothy 2:2). To Philemon he wrote that he was remembering him in his prayers because of his love and faith in Christ and that he would be active in sharing his faith. He especially was praying for Onesimus, a wayward slave who had trusted in the Lord after escaping, but now was being sent back by Paul (Philemon 4-11). He prayed and sang praises with Silas when they were imprisoned unjustly, and God delivered them (Acts 16:25-34). He prayed for all aboard ship bound for Rome who were endangered of perishing. The Lord told him that all would be saved, and he believed what God had told him, and all were spared (Acts 27:21-25). When they were beached on the island of Malta, he prayed for the father of the chief official and others who were sick there, and they were healed. However, when he asked the Lord three times to remove a thorn in his flesh, the Lord did not remove it, but instead gave him grace to live with it. God's strength is made perfect in weakness (2 Corinthians 12:1-10). To the Ephesians he wrote to take up the armor of God and pray in the Spirit on all occasions and be alert, praying for all the saints always (Ephesians 6:18). Then he prayed this personal prayer:

> Pray also for me, that whenever I open my mouth, words may be given me so that I will fearlessly make known the mystery of the gospel, for which I am an

ambassador in chains. Pray that I may declare it fearlessly, as I should (Ephesians 6:19-20).

Here is an appeal relating preaching and prayer.

After his conversion, Paul struggled to keep in the center of God's will, and eventually he served wholeheartedly according to God's direction. He gained the victory through the Spirit and prayer (Philippians 1:19). The spiritual battles were difficult, often through persecution and suffering, but he proclaimed the word of God with boldness and great power throughout much of the Roman world.

CHAPTER III

HIS MESSAGES

Following his conversion, Saul was led to Damascus where Ananias was called to commission him as a chosen instrument to carry the name of Christ to the Gentiles and their kings and before the people of Israel. Ananias laid his hands on Saul who then received his sight, was filled with the Holy Spirit, and was baptized. Shortly thereafter, he was strengthened and began to preach in the synagogues that Jesus is the Son of God. He grew more and more powerful, proving that Jesus is the Christ (Acts 9:20-22).

Several words are used for the proclamation of the word of God. The word "preaching" in the Greek language is *kerygma* and means the message of public proclamation and is not how the preacher acts in his delivery. The other word used most often in Scripture is "evangelizing," *euangelion*, which is often translated preaching the gospel, but means good news, namely, the death, burial, and resurrection of Christ (1 Corinthians 15:1-4). This was the basic truth behind Paul's messages, whether his sermons, the defense of the faith, witnessing, or other means of proclamation. Though the above words and their derivatives to preach (*kerussein*) and to preach the gospel (*euangelizesthai*) are used most often by Paul, he also used other words of proclamation, such as the words to speak (*lalein*), to exhort (*parakalein*), to witness (*marturein*), to prophesy (*propheteuein*), and to teach (*didaskein*).

Later Paul came to Jerusalem after escaping the Jews who conspired to kill him. However, the disciples were fearful of him, not convinced that he was a true disciple. Barnabas took him to the apostles and told them how he had seen the Lord on the road to Damascus and spoke to him (Acts 9:23-27). Paul stayed in Jerusalem and moved about freely, and he continued to speak boldly in Jesus' name and to debate the Grecian Jews. Again the Jewish leaders tried to kill him. When the leaders of the disciples heard this, they took him to Caesarea and then sent him off to Tarsus. The churches in Judea, Galilee, and Samaria were strengthened and encouraged by the Holy Spirit, growing in numbers and living in the fear of the Lord (Acts 9:28-31).

Message in Pisidian Antioch

Peter was successful at Caesarea in the leading the devout and God-fearing Gentile Cornelius to Christ. He realized through visions that the Lord granted the Gentiles repentance unto life. Moreover, the disciples who had been scattered because of persecution took the message to the Jews throughout the land. Some of them spoke to the Gentiles, and a great number of these believed. When the leaders of the church at Jerusalem heard this, they sent Barnabas to Antioch of Syria. He saw the evidence that the hand of the Lord was on the Gentiles, for a great number turned to him by faith. Barnabas then traveled to Tarsus and brought Paul to Antioch. Then the church there set apart Barnabas and Paul to their first missionary journey (Acts 13:1-3). After traveling through Cyprus to Paphos in Asia Minor preaching the word, they traveled on to Perga preaching the word of God along the way with effectiveness. They arrived at Antioch of Pisidia where they proclaimed the gospel. The first recorded message in the book of Acts is provided here (Acts 13:13-14). On the Sabbath they entered the Jewish synagogue. After the law and the prophets were read, the rulers asked whether they had a word of encouragement and let them speak. Paul took the opportunity. Standing up, he motioned with his hand and said:

> Men of Israel and you Gentiles who worship God, listen to me! The God of the people of Israel chose our fathers; he made the people prosper during their stay in Egypt, with mighty power he led them out of that country, he endured their conduct for about forty years in the desert, he overthrew seven nations in Canaan and gave their land to his people as their inheritance. All this took about 450 years.
>
> After this, God gave them judges until the time of Samuel the prophet. Then the people asked for a king, and he gave them Saul son of Kish, of the tribe of Benjamin, who ruled forty years. After removing Saul, he made David their king. He testified concerning him: 'I have found David son of Jesse a man after my own heart; he will do everything I want him to do.'
>
> From this man's descendants God has brought to Israel the Savior Jesus, as he promised. Before the coming of Jesus, John preached repentance and baptism to all the people of Israel. As John was completing his work, he said: 'Who do you think I am? I am not that one. No, but he is coming after me, whose sandals I am not worthy to untie.'
>
> Brothers, children of Abraham, and you God-fearing Gentiles, it is to us that this message of salvation has been sent. The people of Jerusalem and their rulers did not recognize Jesus, yet in condemning him they fulfilled the words of the prophets that are read every Sabbath. Though they found no proper ground for a death sentence, they asked Pilate to have him executed. When they had carried out all that was written about him, they took him down from the tree and laid him in a tomb. But God raised him from the dead, and for many days he was seen by those who had traveled with him from Galilee to Jerusalem. They are now his witnesses to our people.
>
> We tell you the good news: What God promised our fathers he has fulfilled for us, their children, by raising up Jesus. As it is written in the second Psalm:
> 'You are my Son; today I have become your Father.'
> The fact that God raised him from the dead, never to decay, is stated in these words:
> 'I will give you the holy and sure blessings promised to David.'
> So it is stated elsewhere:
> 'You will not let your Holy One see decay.'
> For when David had served God's purpose in his own generation, he fell

asleep; he was buried with his fathers and his body decayed. But the one whom God raised from the dead did not see decay.

Therefore, my brothers, I want you to know that through Jesus the forgiveness of sins is proclaimed to you. Through him everyone who believes is justified from everything you could not be justified from by the law of Moses. Take care that what the prophets have said does not happen to you:

'Look, you scoffers, wonder and perish, for I am going to do something in your days that you would never believe, even if someone told you' (Acts 13:16-41).

This was the record of Paul's message, written by Luke inspired by the Holy Spirit for the word of God for posterity. The message may be analyzed as follows:

Introduction: Paul began by motioning with his hand and calling on the men of Israel and the Gentiles to listen.

First: He reviewed briefly God's concern and care for his people from the time of their stay in Egypt and the exodus under Moses' leadership to the ministry of John the Baptist and his call to repentance and baptism.

Second: He proclaimed the message of salvation during which Jesus the Messiah is condemned to death as the prophets had predicted and laid in a tomb.

Third: He told how God raised up Jesus from the dead and how he was seen many days as prophesied, citing several Old Testament passages.

Conclusion: He made an appeal for faith to receive the forgiveness of sins through Jesus and told that men are justified from everything that could not be justified by the law of Moses. He then warned them not to be like scoffers who would not believe and perished.

After the message Paul and Barnabas left the synagogue and were invited to speak again the next Sabbath. Many of the Jews and the devout Jewish converts followed them and listened as they discussed the message. They were urged to continue in the grace of God. The next Sabbath many of the Jewish leaders saw the crowds and were filled with jealousy and talked abusively against what Paul had said. Paul and Barnabas replied boldly, saying, "We had to speak the word of God to you first. Since you reject it and do not consider yourselves worthy of eternal life, we now turn to the Gentiles. For this is what the Lord has commanded us" (Acts 13:46-47). They cited Isaiah 49:6. When the Gentiles heard this, they were glad and honored the word of God. All of who were appointed to eternal life believed his word.

The core of the gospel was proclaimed in this message by Paul: "Christ died for our sins according to the Scriptures, that he was buried, that he was raised on the third day according to the Scriptures" (1 Corinthians 15:3-4). He could have cited many Old Testament passages, such as Isaiah 53 and Psalm 16:8-11, to support his message effectively. He discussed his message after he delivered it to them since many were Jews and devout Gentile converts to Judaism.

So Paul and Barnabas spread the word of God throughout southeastern Asia Minor winning some Jews and many Gentiles. They returned to Antioch of Syria and reported all they accomplished through the grace of God. Having resolved the question on how the Gentiles are saved by grace alone and not required to keep the law of Moses, Paul embarked on his second missionary journey with Silas across Asia Minor and into Europe. Again the Lord blessed their efforts of preaching the gospel to the Greeks at Philippi, Thessalonica, and Berea.

Message in Athens

Paul left Silas and Timothy at Berea and traveled to Athens. He was distressed over the city full of idols. He reasoned with the Jews and the God-fearing Greeks in the marketplace. A group of Epicureans and Stoic philosophers began to debate with him regarding the resurrection of the dead. They said that he was advocating foreign gods because Paul was preaching the good news about Jesus and the resurrection. They brought him to a meeting at the Aeropagus wanting to know more of this new teaching. For they spent much of their time talking and listening to new ideas (Acts 17:16-21). They gave Paul an opportunity to speak. He stood up in the meeting and said:

> Men of Athens! I see that in every way you are very religious. For as I walked around and looked carefully at your objects of worship, I even found an altar with this inscription: TO AN UNKNOWN GOD. Now what you worship as something unknown I am going to proclaim to you.
> The God who made the world and everything in it is the Lord of heaven and earth and does not live in temples built by hands. And he is not served by human hands, as if he needed anything, because he himself gives all men life and breath and everything else. From one man he made every nation of men, that they should inhabit the whole earth; and he determined the times set for them and the exact places where they should live. God did this so that men would seek him and perhaps reach out for him and find him, though he is not far from each one of us. For in him we live and move and have our being. As some of your own poets have said, 'We are his offspring.'
> Therefore since we are God's offspring, we should not think that the divine being is like gold or silver or stone—an image made of man's design and skill. In the past God overlooked such ignorance, but now he commands all people everywhere to repent. For he has set a day when he will judge the world with justice by the man he has appointed. He has given proof of this to all men by raising him from the dead (Acts 17:22-31).

Paul organized this message as follows:
Introduction: He introduced his message by referring to an inscription on an altar TO AN UNKNOWN GOD and noting that they were very religious, beginning where they were in their understanding.
First: He proceeded to proclaim that the God who made the world and everything in it is the Lord of heaven and earth and does not live in man-made temples. He gives life and breath and everything else.

Second: He said that from one man he made all nations of men to inhabit the earth and determined the times and places where they should live, and perhaps they would seek him and find him, citing one of their poets.

Third: He reminded them that they were God's offspring and should not think the divine being is made through man's skill, an image made of gold, silver, or stone.

Conclusion: He concluded by making an appeal that since God overlooked their ignorance, people everywhere should repent, since God will judge the world by the man that he appointed. The proof of this is that God raised Jesus from the dead.

When they heard about the resurrection from the dead, some sneered, but others said we want to hear more of this. A few men including Dionysius, a member of the Aeropagus, responded and became Paul's followers believing in the Lord. A prominent woman Damaris also became a follower. They believed that Jesus was the man that Paul was talking about in his message because they heard him preaching about Jesus and the resurrection (Acts 17:32-34). Here again we have Paul's sermon, recorded by Luke, and reported by him in his history of the early church as the Spirit of God directed.

Paul continued to minister and proclaim the good news in Greece, including a significant ministry in Corinth, and also in Ephesus in western Asia Minor. He established churches, ordained ministers, and spoke words of encouragement to the disciples throughout these areas, and returned to Antioch.

Message in Miletus

After spending some time in Antioch, he traveled again through Asia Minor evangelizing and also strengthening churches. He arrived at Ephesus and spent over two years there, spreading the word of God to Jews and Greeks who lived in its province. After a riot in Ephesus, he traveled through Macedonia and Greece speaking words of encouragement, but with continued controversy. He raised a collection for the poor saints in Jerusalem and then decided to leave there and to pass by Ephesus. He sent for the elders of the church at Ephesus to meet him at Miletus. When they arrived, he delivered the following pastoral message:

> You know how I lived the whole time I was with you, from the first day I came into the province of Asia. I served the Lord with great humility and with tears, although I was severely tested by the plots of the Jews. You know that I would not have hesitated to preach anything that would be helpful to you but have taught you publicly and from house to house. I have declared to both Jews and Greeks that they must turn to God in repentance and have faith in our Lord Jesus.
>
> And now, compelled by the Spirit, I am going to Jerusalem, not knowing what will happen to me there. I only know that in every city the Holy Spirit warns me that prison and hardships are facing me. However, I consider my life worth nothing to me, if only I may finish the race and complete the task the Lord

> Jesus has given me—the task of testifying to the gospel of God's grace.
> Now I know that none of you among whom I have gone about preaching the kingdom will ever see me again. Therefore, I declare to you today that I am innocent of the blood of all men. For I have not hesitated to proclaim to you the whole will of God. Keep watch over yourselves and all the flock of which the Holy Spirit has made you overseers. Be shepherds of the church of God, which he bought with his own blood. I know that after I leave, savage wolves will come in among you and will not spare the flock. Even from your own number men will arise and distort the truth in order to draw away disciples after them. So be on your guard! Remember that for three years I never stopped warning each of you night and day with tears.
> Now I commit you to God and to the word of his grace, which can build you up and give you an inheritance among all those who are sanctified. I have not coveted anyone's silver or gold or clothing. You yourselves know that these hands of mine have supplied my own needs and the needs of my companions. In everything I did, I showed you that by this kind of hard work we must help the weak, remembering the words the Lord Jesus himself said: 'It is more blessed to give than to receive.' (Acts 20:18-35).

When he had said this, he knelt down with all of them and prayed. They all wept when they embraced him and kissed him. What grieved them most was his statement that they would never see his face again. Then they accompanied him to the ship.

His message may be organized as follows:

Introduction: He reminded them of his faithful service to them in preaching the word of God to Jews and Greeks that they would repent toward God and have faith in Christ.

First: He is being called to Jerusalem by the Spirit and is committed to the task of testifying to the gospel of grace.

Second: He would not see them again, but he had not neglected anyone, not hesitating to proclaim the whole will of God.

Third: He warned them that men would come after him and scatter the disciples who were bought by the blood. They are to be good shepherds and guard the church of God.

Conclusion: He commended them to the word of God's grace. He had not coveted their wealth, but had supplied his own needs and his companions and helped the weak, and he reminded them of the words of the Lord Jesus, "It is more blessed to give than receive."

Then he knelt down and prayed for them, embracing them with affection. They had been fellow-servants of the Lord through difficult years and grieved that they would not see him again as they accompanied him to the ship. This sketch of his message on the gospel of grace includes a statement regarding repentance toward God and faith in Jesus Christ. He then left them on his final trip to Jerusalem via Syria and Tyre.

Message in Jerusalem

Paul was received warmly by the brethren and reported how the Gentiles were receptive to the word of God through his ministry. But the Jews and their leaders stirred up the crowds so that city was aroused, thinking that Paul desecrated the temple by bringing in Greek Christians. A mob dragged him from the temple and were about to kill him, but he was rescued by the governor's soldiers. He asked the commander to let him speak in his defense. When he received permission, Paul stood up on the steps of the barracks and motioned to the crowd. When they became silent, he spoke his message in Aramaic:

> I am a Jew, born in Tarsus of Cilicia, but brought up in this city. Under Gamaliel I was thoroughly trained in the law of our fathers and was just as zealous for God as any of you are today. I persecuted the followers of this Way to their death, arresting both men and women and throwing them in prison, as also the high priest and all the Council can testify. I even obtained letters from them to their brothers in Damascus, and went there to bring these people as prisoners to Jerusalem to be punished.
> About noon as I came near Damascus, suddenly a bright light from heaven flashed around me. I fell to the ground and heard a voice say to me, 'Saul! Saul! Why do you persecute me?'
> 'Who are you, Lord?' I asked.
> 'I am Jesus of Nazareth, whom you are persecuting,' he replied. My companions saw the light, but they did not understand the voice of him who was speaking to me.
> 'What shall I do, Lord?' I asked.
> 'Get up,' the Lord said, 'and go into Damascus. There you will be told all that you have been assigned to do.' My companions led me by the hand into Damascus, because the brilliance of the light had blinded me.
> A man named Ananias came to see me. He was a devout observer of the law and highly respected by all the Jews living there. He stood beside me and said, 'Brother Saul, receive your sight!' And at that very moment I was able to see him.
> Then he said: 'The God of our fathers has chosen you to know his will and to see the Righteous One and to hear words from his mouth. You will be his witness to all men of what you have seen and heard. And now what are you waiting for? Get up, be baptized and wash your sins away, calling on his name.'
> When I returned to Jerusalem and was praying at the temple, I fell into a trance and saw the Lord speaking. 'Quick!' he said to me, 'Leave Jerusalem immediately, because they will not accept your testimony about me.'
> 'Lord,' I replied, 'these men know that I went from one synagogue to another to imprison and beat those who believe in you. And when the blood of your martyr Stephen was shed, I stood there giving my approval and guarding the clothes of those who were killing him.'
> Then the Lord said to me, 'Go; I will send you far away to the Gentiles.' (Acts 22:3-21).

This message may be organized as follows:

Introduction: He introduced himself briefly as a Jew born in Cilicia and brought up there.

First: He described his past life and instruction under Gamaliel and explained how jealous he was for the Jewish laws, leading to the persecution of the church.

Second: He described his conversion on the road to Damascus and meeting the Lord in a climactic experience, and then his encounter with Ananias in which he received his sight again.

Third: He described his calling as one chosen to see the Lord and received the call to be his witness.

Conclusion: He concluded by telling of his difficulty in his beginning ministry among the Jews, but also telling how the Lord sent him away to the Gentiles.

The crowd listened intently until he said that his mission was to the Gentiles. Then they cried out to kill him. A great uproar occurred, but the commander rescued him. When he heard that Paul was a Roman citizen and was warned of a plot to kill him, the commander sent him to Caesarea.

Messages in Caesarea

Paul delivered two messages in Caesarea. First of all the accusers including the high priest and the elders were summoned by Governor Felix to bring charges against Paul in Caesarea. Their spokesman named Tertullus charged that he was a troublemaker, stirring up riots, a ringleader of the Nazarene sect and desecrater of the temple. The governor then allowed Paul to respond to the charges, and he replied as follows:

> I know that for a number of years you have been a judge over this nation; so I gladly make my defense. You can easily verify that no more than twelve days ago I went up to Jerusalem to worship. My accusers did not find me arguing with anyone at the temple, or stirring up a crowd in the synagogues or anywhere else in the city. And they cannot prove to you the charges they are now making against me. However, I admit that I worship the God of our fathers as a follower of the Way, which they call a sect. I believe everything that agrees with the Law and that is written in the Prophets, and I have the same hope in God as these men, that there will be a resurrection of both the righteous and the wicked. So I strive always to keep my conscience clear before God and man.
>
> After an absence of several years, I came to Jerusalem to bring my people gifts for the poor and to present offerings. I was ceremonially clean when they found me in the temple courts doing this. There was no crowd with me, nor was I involved in any disturbance. But there are some Jews from the province of Asia, who ought to be here before you and bring charges if they have anything against me. Or these who are here should state what crime they found in me when I stood before the Sanhedrin—unless it was this one thing I shouted as I stood in their presence: 'It is concerning the resurrection of the dead that I am on trial before you today.' (Acts 24:10-21).

Paul's defense may be arranged as follows:

Introduction: He acknowledged that the governor had been a judge over the nation and was glad to make a defense before him.

First: They could verify his behavior in Jerusalem and find that he was not arguing with anyone and stirring up a crowd.

Second: He admitted that he worships the God of the fathers as a follower of the Way and in agreement with the Law and the Prophets.

Third: He had the same hope as the accusers that there will be a resurrection of the dead of both the righteous and the wicked.

Fourth: He came to Jerusalem to bring his people gifts for the poor, he was ceremonially clean, and he was not involved in a disturbance.

Fifth: He asked that the Jews of Asia should be brought forth to bring charges if they have anything against him.

Conclusion: He stated that the only charge against him was his claim concerning the resurrection from the dead.

Governor Felix let the defense stand without further discussion, hoping to receive money from Paul.

After two years Governor Festus succeeded Felix, and when he wanted to send Paul to Jerusalem to appear before the Jewish council, Paul appealed to Caesar. Festus placed the problem before King Agrippa and gathered an assembly to hear Paul's case. With great pomp and ceremony, the assembly was convened, and Paul was allowed to defend himself. Agrippa said to him, "You have permission to speak for yourself." So Paul motioned with his hand and began his defense:

> King Agrippa, I consider myself fortunate to stand before you today as I make my defense against all the accusations of the Jews, and especially so because you are well acquainted with all the Jewish customs and controversies. Therefore, I beg you to listen to me patiently.
>
> The Jews all know the way I have lived ever since I was a child, from the beginning of my life in my own country, and also in Jerusalem. They have known me for a long time and can testify, if they are willing, that according to the strictest sect of our religion, I lived as a Pharisee. And now it is because of my hope in what God has promised our fathers that I am on trial today. This is the promise our twelve tribes are hoping to see fulfilled as they earnestly serve God day and night. O king, it is because of this hope that the Jews are accusing me. Why should any of you consider it incredible that God raises the dead?
>
> I too was convinced that I ought to do all that was possible to oppose the name of Jesus of Nazareth. And that is just what I did in Jerusalem. On the authority of the chief priests I put many of the saints in prison, and when they were put to death, I cast my vote against them. Many a time I went from one synagogue to another to have them punished, and I tried to force them to blaspheme. In my obsession against them, I even went to foreign cities to persecute them.
>
> On one of these journeys I was going to Damascus with the authority and commission of the chief priests. About noon, O king, as I was on the road, I saw a light from heaven, brighter than the sun, blazing around me and my

companions. We all fell to the ground, and I heard a voice saying to me in Aramaic, 'Saul, Saul, why do you persecute me? It is hard for you to kick against the goads.'

Then I asked, 'Who are you, Lord?'

'I am Jesus, whom you are persecuting,' the Lord replied. 'Now get up and stand on your feet. I have appeared to you to appoint you as a servant and as a witness of what you have seen of me and what I will show you. I will rescue you from your own people and from the Gentiles. I am sending you to them to open their eyes and turn them from darkness to light, and from the power of Satan to God, so that they may receive forgiveness of sins and a place among those who are sanctified by faith in me.'

So then, King Agrippa, I was not disobedient to the vision from heaven. First to those in Damascus, then to those in Jerusalem and in all Judea, and to the Gentiles also, I preached that they should repent and turn to God and prove their repentance by their deeds. That is why the Jews seized me in the temple courts and tried to kill me. But I have had God's help to this very day, and so I stand here and testify to small and great alike. I am saying nothing beyond what the prophets and Moses said would happen—that the Christ would suffer and, as the first to rise from the dead, would proclaim light to his own people and to the Gentiles (Acts 26:1-23).

Governor Festus interrupted Paul's defense, claiming that his great learning drove him out of his mind.

Paul arranged his defense in the following manner:

Introduction: He expressed his good fortune of having his defense before the king who was aware of Jewish customs and controversies.

First: He described his background as a Jew and his training and commitment to the strict sect of the Pharisees with the hope promised to the fathers, the hope being accused of, namely, regarding the resurrection of the dead.

Second: He explained why he first opposed Jesus of Nazareth and persecuted his disciples, and this was the reason he was given permission to find them and to put them to death.

Third: He described how he met the Lord on the road to Damascus and committed his life to him in a dramatic conversion experience.

Fourth: He related how he was appointed a witness to the Gentiles, rescuing them from darkness to light that they might receive forgiveness of sins and be set apart by faith in Christ.

Fifth: He stated that he was not disobedient to the vision, but preached that they should repent and turn to God, which was the real reason the Jews attempted to kill him.

Conclusion: He concluded that he had God's help to stand before them, for he had not gone beyond anything that the prophets and Moses said would happen. Moses predicted that the Christ would suffer and rise from the dead, proclaiming light to both Jews and Gentiles.

After he was interrupted by Festus, he appealed to King Agrippa, who was familiar with these things. The king felt that Paul was persuading him to be a

Christian. However, he believed that Paul was innocent of the charges and could be set free except that he had appealed to Caesar. Therefore, he needed to be sent to Rome.

CHAPTER IV

HIS DOCTRINE

At his conversion to Christ, Paul was confronted by the Lord Jesus in a glorious flash of light from heaven. When he asked, "Who are you, Lord?" (Acts 9:5), Jesus told him that he was Jesus of Nazareth whom he was persecuting. Paul acknowledged then that this was the Lord, and he replied, "What shall I do, Lord?" (Acts 22:10). This confession of faith was the basis of the beginning of the proclamation of his message, the word of God.

The Son of God

After he was baptized and filled with the Spirit, Paul began to preach in the synagogues that Jesus is the Son of God, which astonished the Jews because he was the one who was leading in the persecution of the saints. He grew more and more powerful, baffling the Jews there in Damascus, proving that Jesus is the Christ (Acts 9:20-22). These truths were first acknowledged publicly by Peter and the disciples when he confessed to Jesus saying, "You are the Christ, the Son of the living God" (Matthew 16:16). God the Father confirmed this soon thereafter at the Mountain of Transfiguration. Jesus was transfigured before Peter, James, and John, his face shining as the sun and his clothes as a bright light, and the Father saying from a bright cloud, "This is my Son, whom I love; with him I am well-pleased. Listen to him!" (Matthew 17:5).

This fact was the foundational truth to the believing Jews that Jesus is the Jewish Messiah, the Christ. Many of the Jews accepted this as well as a considerable number of the Gentiles in Damascus. When he had to flee from the city because the Jewish leaders rejected his claims and sought to kill him, he fled to Jerusalem where Barnabas introduced him to the apostles, telling them that the Lord had spoken to him and that he had preached boldly in the name of Jesus. On his first missionary journey in Antioch of Pisidia, Paul proclaimed that Jesus is the Son of God, citing Psalm 2:7, "You are my Son," proved by the fact that God raised Jesus from the dead (Acts 13:33-34).

Paul elaborated on the deity of Christ in his letter to the Romans. He wrote in his introduction:

> Paul, a servant of Christ Jesus, called to be an apostle and set apart for the gospel of God—the gospel he promised beforehand through his prophets in the Holy Scriptures regarding his Son, who as to his human nature was a descendant of David, and who through the Spirit of holiness was declared with power to be the Son of God by his resurrection from the dead: Jesus Christ our Lord (Romans 1:1-4).

The proof that the Lord Jesus Christ is the Son of God is also shown here by his resurrection from the dead according to the Holy Spirit.

To the Colossians he wrote that the Son of the Father was the image of the invisible God, the first in authority in all creation. He existed before all creation and was creator and sustainer of all things in heaven and earth. Thus he should be given the supremacy (Colossians 1:12-19).

The Gospel and the Cross

Paul specifically proclaimed the gospel, the good news (*euangelion*), when he preached his first recorded message to the people of Antioch of Pisidia. He first surveyed the history of Israel from Moses to John the Baptist, and then he described how Jesus the Messiah fulfilled the promises to the fathers who had prophesied regarding salvation through him. He was rejected by the Jewish leaders and condemned to death as prophesied and laid in a sepulcher, but God raised him from the dead as David predicted and wrote in Psalms 2:7; 16:10. He was seen by many in Jerusalem and Galilee who witnessed his resurrected body. Forgiveness of sins was provided to all who believed in him, with a warning to those who would not believe and would perish. Many of the Jews and Gentiles believed the message and were persuaded to continue in the grace of God (Acts 13:26-43).

When Paul and Silas arrived in Thessalonica, they went into the synagogue. Paul reasoned with them from the Scriptures, explaining and proving that Christ had to suffer and rise from the dead and that Jesus whom he was proclaiming is the Christ. Many Jews and God-fearing Greeks accepted his message and joined them (Acts 17:1-4). In Caesarea Paul concluded his message before Governor Festus and King Agrippa that Christ must suffer and rise from the dead as the prophets and Moses said would happen (Acts 26:22-23).

These messages confirm what the resurrected Christ told his disciples. To the two disciples on the road to Emmaus, he said, "Did not the Christ have to suffer these thing and then enter his glory?" (Luke 24:26). After this he appeared to the apostles and opened their minds so that they could understand the Scriptures, fulfilling the Law of Moses, the Prophets, and the Psalms. He told them that the Christ would suffer and rise again on the third day and that repentance and forgiveness of sins would be preached in his name to all the nations, beginning at Jerusalem (Luke 24:46-47).

These messages coincide with Paul's statement of the gospel in his first letter to the Corinthians. He wrote:

> Now, brothers, I want to remind you of the gospel I preached to you, which you received and on which you have taken your stand. By this gospel you are saved, if you hold firmly to the word I preached to you. Otherwise, you have believed in vain. For what I received I passed on to you as of first importance: that Christ died for our sins according to the Scriptures, that he was buried, that he was raised on the third day according to the Scriptures, and that he appeared to Peter,

and then to the Twelve. After that, he appeared to more than five hundred of the brothers at the same time, most of whom are still living, though some have fallen asleep. Then he appeared to James, then to all the apostles, and last of all he appeared to me also, as to one abnormally born (1 Corinthians 15:1-8).

Christ died for our sins as Isaiah prophesied (Isaiah 53:12). He rose again as David prophesied (Psalm 2:7; 16:10). Therefore, Paul wrote to the Romans, "But God demonstrates his own love for us in this: While we were still sinners, Christ died for us" (Romans 5:8). Moreover, "He was delivered over to death for our sins and was raised to life for our justification" (Romans 4:25).

The gospel, meaning good news, was preached to the Corinthians; they received it and were saved (1 Corinthians 15:1-2). Paul was ready to preach the gospel to the Romans, for "it is the power of God for the salvation of everyone who believes: first for the Jew, then for the Gentile" (Romans 1:16). This gospel was proclaimed by Paul over much of the Roman world in the first century.

The Gospel and the Resurrection

In the recorded messages of Paul, he gives particular emphasis to the resurrection of Christ. He stated in his first letter to the Corinthians that while he was with them, he was determined not to know anything among them except Jesus Christ and him crucified, revealing his emphasis on the necessity of Christ's death for sin (1 Corinthians 2:2). The truth of this central fact depends upon the resurrection of Christ from the grave, which declared him to be the Son of God with power by this resurrection for salvation to everyone who believes (Romans 1:4,16). In his message to the Jews of Antioch of Pisidia, he declared that the gospel fulfilled the promise made to the fathers by the resurrection from the dead, providing forgiveness of sins to those that believe (Acts 13:32-39). In his message to the Greeks at the Areopagus in Athens, he preached that God had appointed a day when he would judge the world in righteousness by the man he ordained named Jesus. He gave assurance of this by raising him from the dead (Acts 17:31). Some mocked, but others wanted to hear more about this matter, and a few joined the disciples.

In his defense before the Jewish council in Jerusalem, Paul testified to seeing the resurrected Christ and committed his life to him. He made his plea on the hope of the resurrection from the dead. This caused a division among the leaders. However, the Pharisees, who believed in the resurrection of the dead, supported Paul's plea (Acts 23:6-9). Furthermore, in his message before Governor Festus and King Agrippa, he testified that Christ would suffer and be the first to rise from the dead and would proclaim light to the Jews and the Gentiles (Acts 26:22-23).

Thus, his emphasis in these messages to unbelievers in his audiences was on the resurrection of Christ as the undeniable proof of the power and effectiveness of the gospel as stated in the word of God.

Paul wrote in his first letter to the Corinthians about the reality and necessity of the resurrection of Christ. He and others preached that Christ had truly been raised from the dead. He reasoned:

> But if it is preached that Christ has been raised from the dead, how can some of you say that there is no resurrection of the dead? If there is no resurrection of the dead, then not even Christ has been raised. And if Christ has not been raised, our preaching is useless and so is your faith. More than that, we are then found to be false witnesses about God, for we have testified about God that he raised Christ from the dead. But he did not raise him if in fact the dead are not raised. For if the dead are not raised, then Christ has not been raised either. And if Christ has not been raised, your faith is futile; you are still in your sins. Then those also who have fallen asleep in Christ are lost. If only for this life we have hope in Christ, we are to be pitied more than all men. But Christ has indeed been raised from the dead, the firstfruits of those who have fallen asleep (1 Corinthians 15:12-20).

His whole argument in 1 Corinthians was based on the fact of the resurrection of Christ from the dead, an absolute necessity, and the encouragement of Christians. For they have this blessed hope of the second coming of Christ when this mortal body will put on immortality. "Thanks be to God! He gives us the victory through our Lord Jesus Christ," he declared (1 Corinthians 15:57). Thus we understand why the resurrection of Christ was so prominent in Paul's messages in the book of Acts and in his supporting statements in his letters.

Salvation through Faith in Christ

Salvation through faith in Christ is the emphasis in Paul's recorded messages by which he sought to reach both Jews and Gentiles. His messages reveal the meaning of the gospel: justification by faith and not by keeping the law, the righteous living by faith, and salvation offered to everyone, whether Jew or Gentile. These truths are revealed in his theme in the book of Romans stated in his introduction:

> I am not ashamed of the gospel, because it is the power of God for the salvation of everyone who believes: first for the Jew, then for the Gentile. For in the gospel a righteousness from God is revealed, a righteousness that is by faith from first to last, just as it is written: 'The righteous will live by faith' (Romans 1:16-17; Habakkuk 2:4).

These truths appear in his first recorded message in Antioch of Pisidia. He first surveyed God's work with his people Israel, and then appealed to the descendants of Abraham and God-fearing Gentiles, saying the word of salvation has been sent to you. He presented the gospel to them, declaring that Jesus was crucified and resurrected, providing forgiveness of sins to everyone who believes. They are justified from all things that could not be justified by the law of Moses (Acts 13:26-39). When the Gentiles heard this, they were glad and glorified the word of God.

HIS DOCTRINE 33

Those who were appointed to eternal life believed (Acts 13:48).

When Paul and Barnabas returned to Antioch in Syria where they were first appointed, they reported how God had opened the door of salvation to the Gentiles. Some time later several Judaizers came there and said that unless Gentiles are circumcised according to the custom of Moses, they cannot be saved (Acts 15:1). A dispute arose over the matter; so the church sent them to Jerusalem to discuss the matter with the apostles and elders. They reported on all the things God had done through them in opening the door to the Gentiles. The testimony of Peter led to a resolution of the conflict, the council deciding that all people are saved in the same manner. James reported that they should not trouble the Gentiles who were turning to God with having to be circumcised and keeping other regulations of the law of Moses (Acts 15:12-21).

During the second missionary journey, Paul and Silas preached the gospel in Macedonia. During their ministry in Philippi, an uproar occurred because of their work, and they were thrown into prison. During an earthquake the prison doors were opened. When the jailor feared the prisoners had escaped, he was about to kill himself. Paul called out to him not to harm himself. He fell down trembling, asking "What must I do to be saved?" They replied, "Believe in the Lord Jesus, and you will be saved—you and your household." They spoke the word of the Lord to him and the others in his household, who believed in God and rejoiced, and were baptized. Here is a clear incident indicating that people are saved through faith in Christ (Acts 16:25-34).

Paul made this truth clearly and distinctly in his letter to the Ephesians, stating:

> For it is by grace you have been saved, through faith—and this not from yourselves, it is the gift of God—not by works, so that no one can boast. For we are God's workmanship, created in Christ Jesus to do good works, which God prepared in advance for us to do (Ephesians 2:8-10).

People are saved by grace through faith, not of works, but in Christ are called to do good works for him. Paul summed up the word of faith, which he proclaimed in his letter to the Romans, writing:

> 'The word is near you; it is in your mouth and in your heart,' that is, the word of faith we are proclaiming. That if you confess with your mouth, 'Jesus is Lord,' and believe in your heart that God raised him from the dead, you will be saved. For it is with your heart that you believe and are justified, and it is with your mouth that you confess and are saved (Romans 10:8-10).

Paul preached Jesus and the resurrection to the Greeks at the Aeropagus in Athens. They had little or no background knowledge as his Jewish audiences and claimed that he preached foreign gods. But he pointed to their worship at the altar TO THE UNKNOWN GOD. He proclaimed the living God who created the world and gives life and breath and all things. He appealed to them to repent from their worship of idols, for God overlooks their ignorance and has appointed a day in which he will judge the world by Jesus whom he resurrected. Many mocked Paul, but some had faith and followed him.

In his last recorded message in Jerusalem, Paul gave his testimony of his early life and his persecution of the church, and then told of his meeting the Lord and committing his life to him. He explained his calling to proclaim the word to the Jews but primarily to the Gentiles to open their eyes that they would turn from darkness to light and from the power of Satan to God. Then they would receive forgiveness of sins and an inheritance among those that are set apart by faith in Christ. He closed with a presentation of the gospel of Christ who suffered unto death and rose from the grave for both Jews and Gentiles, granting salvation to all who had faith in Christ.

The Work of God in History

In Paul's recorded messages in Acts, he emphasized God's plan and activities in history. This was especially true in messages when the audience was primarily Jews in the synagogues in the Roman empire and in Israel. He had to show and prove that Jesus was descended from Abraham and was the fulfillment of the prophesies from Moses to the latter prophets as Paul's references indicated. This proof was essential to win the Jews' acceptance of Jesus and the gospel. In his messages to the Gentiles, he had to approach them from their background which was both philosophical and inquisitive as revealed in his message to the Greeks at the Aeropagus.

For example, in Paul's message to the Jews at Antioch, he reminded them of the historical background of the people of Israel, from their captivity and deliverance in Egypt to the ministry of John the Baptist. This led to his proclamation of the crucifixion and resurrection of Christ as predicted by the prophets. Then he made his appeal for the forgiveness of sins through Christ to everyone who believes, who are justified from all things that could not be justified by the law of Moses. He warned them not to despise God's offer of salvation, which was foretold by the prophets. Thus, in this message a brief survey of the history of Israel laid the foundation of the coming of the Messiah and his work of redemption. This information, inspiration, and warning was needed by the Jews and proselytes to find salvation through faith in Christ. Many of the Jews and also the Gentiles accepted the message and believed God's work in the world and trusted in Christ (Acts 13:16-41).

Pastoral Care

In Miletus Paul's message to the elders of the church at Ephesus provides insight on how he related to ministers and other leaders. He first reminded them in brief statements about how he lived and how he served with them as examples of leadership. He mentioned the following ways:

He served with humility and tears.
He was severely tested by plots against him.
He taught them publicly and in their homes.
He declared to Jews and Gentiles to repent and have faith in Christ.
He told them that he was leaving them and facing hardships.
He hoped to complete his task of testifying to the gospel of God's grace.
He was innocent of the blood of all men.

Then he charged the elders with the following tasks:
Keep watch over yourselves and the flock given to you as overseers.
Be good shepherds of the church, for wolves will come and scatter the flock.
Watch out for men who distort the truth and draw away disciples.

He closed his message by committing them to God and the word of his grace that would build them up and give them an inheritance. He reminded them that he did not covet their wealth, but worked with his hands to provide for his needs. And they should remember the words of the Lord who said, "It is more blessed to give than receive." (Acts 20:17-35).

He set an example for Christian life and service before them, especially as the leaders of the church. Then he reminded these elders of the important principles of service for the Lord. He urged them to accept the challenges that would come after he was gone and concluded with an important word from the Lord Jesus about giving and receiving in stewardship.

The pastoral letters of Timothy and Titus provide a wealth of information regarding pastoral work and care, the lives of pastors and other leaders, and the life and ministry of churches. Additional information and help is scattered throughout his other letters regarding these matters.

Paul spent some thirty-five years of ministry and of preaching, and no doubt preached and taught many of these great truths on many occasions according to the needs of the churches and ministers. Many other major doctrines are mentioned in his letters that are not covered in his recorded messages. These are the doctrines of revelation, God, creation, man and sin, the Holy Spirit, reconciliation, justification, sanctification, last things, the church, and Christian life and service in detail. Some of these will appear in later discussions on his instructions on preaching.

CHAPTER V

HIS ORGANIZATION OF MESSAGES

The six messages recorded in the book of Acts do not give many details as to how Paul organized his messages, but do provide some principles as to the structure of them. He no doubt gave many lengthy messages as Luke indicates in the book of Acts (Acts 13:42-43; 20:7-12). However, these are Luke's reports as the Holy Spirit inspired this author concerning such messages as sermons, homilies, instructions, speeches, defenses, and other ways of communicating the word of God.

The Foundation of the Messages

These messages may be classified as topical messages, that is the topic or subject is drawn from the purpose of Paul in the light of the needs of the audience, whether it is primarily to Jews, or to Gentiles, or to both. In these messages the following information is indicated:

In Antioch of Pisidia (Acts 13:16-41):
Subject: " The Promised Messiah of History Has Come."
The setting is the Sabbath day in the synagogue, and the audience was primarily Jews and God-fearing Gentiles. Paul and Barnabas were visiting Jews, and after the reading of the Law and the prophets they were then invited to speak any word of encouragement, as was probably their custom.

In Athens (Acts 17:16-31):
Subject: "The Unknown God Made Himself Known."
The setting was the meeting at the Aeropagus in Athens after Paul had reasoned with the Jews and God-fearing Greeks in the synagogue and in the market place day by day. A group of Epicureans and Stoic philosophers disputed with him, wondering what this babbler was saying, proclaiming foreign gods, preaching about Jesus Christ and the resurrection. The Athenians and foreigners were particularly interested in new doctrines, and they spent much time talking about these matters. They gave Paul the opportunity to speak about his new doctrines.

In Miletus (Acts 20:17-38):
Subject: "Live before Men in Dedicated Service for the Lord."
The setting was a called meeting in Miletus of the elders of the church of Ephesus. His audience was primarily the leaders of the church. Paul was in a hurry on his way to Jerusalem in order to be there on the day of Pentecost. He knew this would be his last opportunity to speak to these leaders whom he led to Christ and ordained to the ministry. Other leaders and brethren were probably with them.

In Jerusalem (Acts 21:37-22:22):
Subject: "Christ Saved Me and Called Me to Reach the Gentiles."
The setting was a violent mob of Jews who stirred up the people to kill Paul, but he

38 HIS ORANIZATION OF MESSAGES

was delivered by Roman soldiers. Paul then asked to speak to the crowd. The commander of the Roman soldiers allowed him to speak in his own defense before the Jews who were intent on what he would say in order to convict him all the more.

In Caesarea (Acts 24:10-21; 26:1-32):

Subjects: "Christ Saved Me and Called Me to a World Mission."

The settings were gatherings of leaders called by the Roman governors Felix and Festus before prominent Jewish and Roman officials to hear Paul's defense and provide information to write to Caesar concerning the charges against him. The audiences were antagonistic Jewish leaders and concerned Roman officials about the real issue and the message to be sent to Rome since Paul appealed to Caesar.

In these messages Paul met a real need as he usually did in his private and public conversations, proclamations, and writings. He set an example for all who ministered and proclaimed the word of God. The messages at Jerusalem were extremely important to the early church, but also to the church down through the centuries. They confirm Paul's conversion and calling to a world mission providing salvation to all who call on Christ for salvation, both Jews and Gentiles.

The Introduction of the Messages

In each of the recorded messages, Paul introduced them in a manner based on the occasion, the need, the revelation of Old Testament Scriptures, and the direction of the inspiration of the Spirit.

In Antioch of Pisidia, he took advantage of the offer of the synagogue rulers to give a word of encouragement. He first of all stood, which was unusual since sitting was the custom, and motioned with his hand to gain the attention of his audience. Following the reading of the Scriptures, he addressed them courteously, saying, "Men of Israel and you Gentiles who worship God, listen to me!" He began with the record of God's dealing with the people of Israel as recorded in the Pentateuch and especially the Law of Moses. With this introduction he moved into a detailed survey of the lives of people of the nation of Israel (Acts 13:15-25).

In Athens, Paul stood in the midst of the meeting of the Areopagus. He then addressed those assembled as "Men of Athens," and commented on their religious nature. Then he called attention to the altar with the inscription "TO AN UNKNOWN GOD," and proceeded to say that "what you worship as something unknown I am going to proclaim to you." He is the God who made the world and everything in it, the Lord of heaven and earth (Acts 17:22-24).

In Miletus when the elders of the church of Ephesus arrived, he reminded these men of his concern for them and how he lived the whole time that he was with them in western Asia Minor. Then he proceeded to tell them the ways he lived and served (Acts 20:17-20).

In Jerusalem he addressed an angry crowd ready to kill him because they thought he brought Greeks into the temple. He wanted to defend his actions and thus asked the Roman commander for permission to speak to them. When allowed to speak and all were silent, he made his defense in Aramaic, the language of the people. He addressed them respectfully, saying, "Brothers and fathers, listen to my defense." When they heard him talking in their common language, they were all attentive, and he began his defense with his testimony (Acts 21:40-22:3).

In Caesarea he was given the opportunity to defend himself before Governors Felix and Festus at a convened court of ranking Jewish and Gentile officials who were respectful and inquisitive regarding the merits of the charges. King Agrippa before Governor Festus' court gave him permission to speak. Paul motioned with his hand to signal his intention to talk. He told his audience that he was fortunate to be able to speak regarding the charges. He told the king that he was especially grateful for his presence since he knew that he was an expert on Jewish customs and questions. He made a plea to them to hear him patiently and was flattered that he was being given a more intense hearing. He again began his messages by giving his testimony (Acts 24:10-11; 26:1-4).

In all these messages Paul understood his audiences and understood the state of mind of the people. He was alert to their current and differing circumstances, and their prejudices and often limited understandings.

The Body of the Messages

The body of the message is the development of the subject of that message, the very core of what the preacher believes the audience needs to hear. The six messages in book of Acts as selected and recorded by Luke, guided and inspired by the Spirit of God, represent ways Paul proclaimed the word of God to people. Luke was not with Paul during his whole ministry, but obtained information from interviews with eye witnesses of the events and from Paul himself during the time he traveled with him (cf. Luke 1:1-4).

In Antioch of Pisidia he developed the subject with two main points to the Jews in the synagogue:
    I. He surveyed God's work with the people of Israel.
    II. He showed how Christ fulfilled what God promised.
In the survey he described how God delivered the people in the Egyptian captivity through Moses. Then he described how God led the people under the judges and kings. He concluded with the ministry of John the Baptist, the forerunner of Jesus the Christ.

In the second half of the message, he presented the fulfillment of what God promised through the gospel of Christ who lived and died under the cruel treatment of the Jewish leaders and Pontus Pilate. He was raised from the dead according to prophesies. Paul cited and interpreted these, moving to an appeal for the acceptance in the conclusion.

In Athens, Paul developed his subject with two points to the skeptical Greeks:
    I. God is the creator of all things and not by idols.
    II. God calls men to repentance, overlooking their ignorance.

In the first part he proclaimed that God is the creator and sustainer of life and all that is heaven and earth, setting boundaries in the world. In the second part he stated that God is not like idols, but overlooked their ignorance. Nevertheless, he reached out to all men, calling on them to repent (Acts 17:24-30).

In Miletus, he developed his message in three parts to the Ephesians elders:
 I. He described his service for the Lord.
 II. He challenged the shepherds of the church to service.
 III. He committed them to God.

He reminded them of his service with them while at Ephesus. In the light of his service, he challenged them to serve likewise, warning of the dangers from others who tried to scatter the flock of believers and distort the truth. Then he committed them to the word of grace and to be good stewards of their wealth in service to others (Acts 20:17-35).

In Jerusalem, he explained to the Jews three aspects of his life in his defense:
 I. He reminded them of his former life as a devout Pharisee.
 II. He described his conversion experience on the road to Damascus.
 III. He told of his calling to be a witness to the Gentiles.

His whole message dealt with his personal experience of salvation and service for the Lord. This was his personal testimony to them, which was needed, but rejected with violence (Acts 22:1-23).

In Caesarea, his messages to the assembly of Jews and Gentiles were organized similarly to the message in Jerusalem:
 I. He lived a life as a devout Pharisee before his conversion.
 II. He described his conversion to Christ on the road to Damascus.
 III. He told of his calling to serve both Jews and especially Gentiles.

He gave more details of his former life and his meeting the Lord on the Damascus road and on his calling to take the gospel to the Gentiles that led to the violent reaction of the Jewish leaders in his defense of the faith (Acts 26:2-23).

The Conclusion of the Messages

After Paul developed his messages, he followed with a conclusion applying the message to the hearts and lives of the persons in the audience. This included an appeal for them to accept God's offer of salvation and service and a warning not to reject his offer. The conclusion then was an invitation to act, an appeal to respond to the gospel for their well-being and God's good pleasure.

In Antioch of Pisidia, he concluded his message to the Jews by presenting Jesus as the one who would forgive the sins of those who believe, being justified from everything that the law of Moses could not do. The response was that he was invited to speak again, with many Jews and proselytes following him. The next Sabbath almost all the people of the city gathered to hear the word of God with a good response to the gospel. But others were jealous and spoke abusively; so then Paul turned to the Gentiles, many of whom were glad and truly believed (Acts 13:39-48).

In Athens, Paul appealed to the Greeks not to think of God as an idol but commanded all men everywhere to reject idolatry and repent. He said that God will set a day to judge the world with justice by Jesus. He gave proof by raising him from the dead. Some sneered but others wanted to hear more of this. A few persons believed and became followers of Paul (Acts 17:22-34).

In Miletus, he concluded his message to the Ephesian elders by reminding them again of his work with them, especially in helping the weak and in remembering the words of the Lord Jesus, "It is more blessed to give than receive." After he said these things, he knelt down with all of them and prayed (Acts 20:35-36).

In Jerusalem, he concluded his message abruptly by telling the antagonistic Jewish crowd what the Lord said to him, "Go; I will send you far away to the Gentiles." When he said this, they shouted, "Rid the earth of him! He's not fit to live!" The Roman commander rescued him from the violent crowd. His message was totally rejected (Acts 22:22-24).

In Caesarea, his first message before Felix was concluded with the decision to delay any action after further consideration and consultation with Paul. Later in his second message before Festus and King Agrippa, he was interrupted by Festus after his third point, who said, "You are out of your mind, Paul!" He shouted, "Your great learning is driving you insane." Paul said that he was not insane, but went on to conclude his message by appealing to King Agrippa, whom he claimed knew the prophets concerning the matters and persuaded him to become a Christian. But the king refused at the time and told Festus that he could be set free, innocent of the charges, but since he appealed to Caesar, he must be sent to him (Acts 26:24-32).

Thus, we see that Paul applied his message to his audience, especially in his conclusions. He appealed to the unbelievers to accept Christ for salvation and forgiveness from sin, based on the gospel. He urged the believers to continue in the faith and serve the Lord with gladness. However, many people rejected his appeals, especially the Jewish leaders. But the Gentiles became more and more receptive to Christ and the gospel.

CHAPTER VI

HIS STYLE OF SPEAKING

The style of a speaker depends on his physical, mental, and psychological qualities, and for the Christian the spiritual qualities. Style includes clarity, force, energy, and imagination, all combined in the way that the speaker develops and delivers his message to his audience. This includes the organization of his message, the arrangement of his thoughts, the use of words and figures of speech, and the use of his voice and actions in delivery.

Natural Abilities

Paul did not have the impressive physical gifts of an orator, for he was probably small in stature and lacked oratorical eloquence. He wrote of the opinion of some others that his bodily presence was unimpressive and his speech was contemptible (2 Corinthians 10:10). Adding to this disadvantage, he had a thorn in the flesh that also affected his ability to speak and kept him humble in appearance (2 Corinthians 12:7-10). However, it did not hinder him from traveling great distances by walking or traveling by donkey or ship. His features were that of the Jew of that time. He wrote to the Galatians with large letters indicating trouble with his eyes in later years that affected his appearance and writing (Galatians 6:11).

But Paul had unusual mental capacity and intellect developed by his training under the tutelage of Gamaliel, the Jewish scholar. He could speak and write in the *koine* Greek language and the common dialect that was the predominant language at the time and was his native tongue. But he also spoke Aramaic, the colloquial language of Palestine through his family and his training in the Jewish culture in Tarsus. His training also included the Hebrew of the Old Testament used in the Jewish liturgy and worship.

However, his strong will led him to be dogmatic and hard-driving. His violent temper was manifested in the persecution of Christians before his conversion experience. Once he came to know Christ personally, some of these traits under God's control became assets. These were manifested at the beginning of his Christian ministry in Israel and Tarsus. In his early missionary journeys, he entered synagogues first in various cities where he preached the word of God with conviction and effectiveness. To the philosophers in Athens, he preached to the skeptical listeners, appealing to their intellect and conscience. On his first trips to Jerusalem and Caesarea, he spoke to the Jews, reasoning with them, in his testimony and the defense of the gospel before Jewish and Gentile leaders. He confounded them proving that Jesus is the Christ as predicted by the prophets. His knowledge of the Old Testament and his skill in debating amazed his audiences and many believed. But most of his listeners there rejected his message because of their prejudices and malicious attitudes.

Spiritual Qualities

The spiritual qualities of the Apostle Paul were far superior to his natural abilities. They did enhance his good natural gifts. They were manifested from the beginning of his Christian conversion when he called upon the name of the Lord on the Damascus road. He was saved and forgiven and became a child of God and a member of the family of God, the church. Shortly thereafter, he was commissioned for service to the world by Christ through Ananias and was baptized and filled with the Holy Spirit. The moment that he was saved, the Spirit of God entered his life. As he wrote to the Ephesians, he was sealed by the Spirit at his conversion, but he also wrote about the command to be filled with the Spirit. This comes by emptying of the believer's life of sin and committing his life to the Lord for power for service (Ephesians 1:13; 4:30; 5:18).

The love of God was shed abroad in his heart, a gift of God (Romans 5:5). This love is the greatest gift, exceeding such gifts as speaking with languages of men and angels, prophesy, understanding mysteries, knowledge, faith that moves mountains, sacrificial giving, and martyrdom. The great gifts are faith, hope, and love, but the greatest gift is love (1 Corinthians 13:1-3, 13).

Paul also received the armor of God that equipped him to withstand struggles against the devil's schemes, flesh and blood, rulers, authorities, and the world (Ephesians 6:10-18). Furthermore, he received the fruit of the Spirit, namely, love, joy, peace, patience, kindness, goodness, faithfulness, gentleness, and self-control that equipped him against the desires of the flesh (Galatians 5:22-26). These spiritual battles were a struggle, especially in the early periods of his life as he wrote in his letter to the Romans (Romans 7:14-25). But he found victory through his total commitment to Christ (Romans 12:1-2). The Spirit of God gave him the victory through the grace given to him to accomplish God's plan for his life (Romans 8:1-17).

Though love is the greatest gift, he did receive other gifts, especially preaching, apostleship, and teaching. His gift of preaching was the first in his calling (1 Timothy 2:7; 2 Timothy 1:11). But he was also called to be an apostle and a teacher of the Gentiles. He was a chosen vessel to carry the Lord's name before the Gentiles, their kings, and the people of Israel and to suffer for his name (Acts 9:15-16). Moreover, he received the support of gifted disciples and preachers such as Luke, Ananias, Barnabas, Silas, Timothy, Titus, and others in his ministry to Jews and Gentiles. Paul sought the prayerful support of these and others as he wrote to the church at Ephesus:

> Pray also for me, that whenever I open my mouth, words may be given me so that I will fearlessly make known the mystery of the gospel, for which I am an ambassador in chains. Pray that I may declare it fearlessly, as I should

(Ephesians 6:19-20).

He wrote to the Corinthians about the great trials and sufferings that he endured, which he was able to bear only through God's grace (2 Corinthians 1:8-11; 4:7-12; 6:3-10; 11:21-30; 12:7-10).

Furthermore, Paul had the word of God, the Holy Scriptures, for his support and encouragement in his ministry. He wrote to Timothy:

> But as for you, continue in what you have learned and have become convinced of, because you know those from whom you learned it, and how from infancy you have known the holy Scriptures, which are able to make you wise for salvation through faith in Christ Jesus. All Scripture is God-breathed and is useful for teaching, rebuking, correcting and training in righteousness, so that the man of God may be thoroughly equipped for every good work (2 Timothy 3:14-17).

Therefore, he charged Timothy to do what he had practiced:

> Preach the Word; be prepared in season and out of season; correct, rebuke and encourage—with great patience and careful instruction. For the time will come when men will not put up with sound doctrine (2 Timothy 4:2-3).

He quoted Scripture to audiences that included Jews and later Gentiles. He believed and proclaimed that the word of God is living and active, sharper than any two-edged sword, penetrating even to the dividing of soul and spirit, and joints and marrow, and it judges the thoughts and attitudes of the heart. Nothing in all creation is hidden from God's sight (Hebrews 4:12-13). He depended on Scripture as the very word of God and the Spirit of God to convict men of sin and lead them to the Savior Jesus Christ.

Clarity of Thought

Paul spoke in the language that his audience understood, whether Aramaic, the colloquial language of the Jews in Palestine, or the *koine* Greek that many in the Roman world understood. They grasped the meaning and the main point of his message, which some understood but many rejected. Some listeners wanted to hear more. He began his ministry by preaching in the synagogues in the city of Damascus, proclaiming that Jesus is the Son of God. Those who heard him were amazed that the man who was persecuting Christians was now preaching the good news of Christ fearlessly. He debated with the Grecian Jews, but many rejected his message and even sought to kill him. He spoke clearly in the language of the people without oratorical devices and eloquence. To the Jews he cited Scripture passages from the Greek Septuagint translation of the Hebrew Old Testament. This was the pattern to Jews in the synagogues as in Antioch in Pisidia. Though many of the Jews understood his message clearly, they rejected the claims of the gospel and stirred up

HIS STYLE OF SPEAKING

persecution. He used words and expressions, sometimes too forthrightly, such as the word "Gentiles," that stirred up antagonistic feelings and raised prejudice and anger in the synagogues. In Athens it was the expression "the resurrection from the dead" that caused the Greek philosophers to mock and sneer. But sooner or later in his messages, these expressions were necessary to reach the hearts and lives of the people.

In Miletus he had a sympathetic audience of Ephesian elders, agreeable with his statements regarding his personal life and ministry during his years of service with them. He spoke personally and passionately with them that kept their attention. In Jerusalem he addressed an antagonistic crowd as he gave his testimony, speaking no doubt in Aramaic. He concluded abruptly with his calling from the Lord to go to the Gentiles with the word. He would probably have been wise to conclude in another manner. However, the Jews were set in their minds to destroy him no matter what he said. In Caesarea he had a more congenial audience, but many of the people were also set on convicting him. The Roman leadership believed in justice according to their laws. Moreover, King Agrippa in hearing Paul and his doctrine, gave him the opportunity to defend himself. He did this capably again with his testimony that could be verified. Again he spoke with no eloquent presentation but with a factual and strait-forward account of his life and ministry.

Paul spoke the truth with clarity in the language of the people with appropriate citations from the Scriptures. The Jews understood what he said whether they believed it or not. Since the events of his conversion and calling occurred in the general area of Syria and adjoining countries, the truth of the facts could be verified. His personal testimony is clearly factual and of keen interest to his hearers and created attention. In his messages Paul began where the people were in their understanding, and as best as he could, he sought to lead them where God wanted them to be through the preaching of the word of God.

Forcefulness of Expression

The message itself and the clarity of thought behind it contribute to the forcefulness of expression. Also, an energetic nature such as Paul's, inspired by the Holy Spirit, is essential to the total impact of the message delivered. Furthermore, the setting and the acoustics are very important. These factors varied in his opportunities to speak to audiences from locations in synagogues to open-air arenas. In Athens the crowd varied in size from a small audience in a portico to a large crowd in the Areopagus. In Miletus the gathering of the elders was small probably in a home or place of business. In Jerusalem the audience was large and in an out-of-doors public place. In Caesarea the location was a large public auditorium. Paul was standing, not sitting, as the custom of a rabbi. His voice was strong without the help of an acoustical device.

Paul on some occasions raised his hand to call attention to him and his message and began to speak with special interest of the audience. He was filled with the

Spirit from the beginning of his preaching of the word of God, motivated by the Spirit as manifested by his boldness and enthusiasm, creating an excitement in the audience. He preached without notes or manuscript and quoted Scripture from memory. He certainly was knowledgeable of events during his conversion and related facts of the region and matters of politics and religion. His arguments in the defense of the truth were often confrontational, especially among antagonistic and skeptical audiences. He spoke with compassion for the lost people to whom he was sent by God's commission. But his heart's desire and prayer was also for the people of Israel that they too might be saved (Romans 10:1). In fact he had great sorrow and anguish of heart for them, even to be cut off from Christ for them (Romans 9:1-4). He was moved to appeal to them to accept Jesus as the Messiah, the Son of God, who died to save them and was raised to justify them (Romans 4:23-25).

In his letter to the Thessalonians, Paul wrote concerning the presentation of the of the gospel and how it should be delivered:

> For we know, brothers loved by God, that he has chosen you, because our gospel came to you not simply with words, but also with power, with the Holy Spirit and with deep conviction. You know how we lived among you for your sake (1 Thessalonians 1:4-5).

Note his emphasis in presenting the gospel:
1. With words
2. With power
3. With the Holy Spirit
4. With deep conviction
5. With an acceptable manner of life

The total impact of these emphases in proclaiming the gospel of Christ gave his presentation great force in his message and in its delivery that moved hearts of people.

Paul's messages were delivered with clarity and force, but with little evidence of elegance, beauty, or the rhetorical skill of an orator. His recorded messages and writings are marked by stylistic grace and learned skill of the Greek language. His theological knowledge and wisdom were both deep and comprehensive. He used imagination and insight in his organization and style in preaching. He took advantage of the uniqueness of the occasions in preaching, such as "To the unknown God" in Athens. He called on the knowledge of King Agrippa in Caesarea. He used the Aramaic language and his Roman citizenship in Jerusalem. Thus, he used what gifts, knowledge, and abilities that he had for Christ and his ministry.

CHAPTER VII

HIS POWER AND EFFECTIVENESS

Shortly after his conversion to Christ, Paul was commissioned a vessel to take the name of Christ to the world. He was sealed with the Holy Spirit as are all Christians at conversion, but he was empowered with the Spirit as commanded by the Lord, as he wrote in his letter to the Ephesians (Ephesians 1:13; 4:30; 5:18). All Christians are indwelt by the Spirit of God, but Paul urged them to be filled with the Spirit, which is the will of God. Paul issued the command "Be filled with the Spirit" to all believers, which is in the passive voice and in continuous action, indicating that it is done by the Lord. Christians must be dedicated to the Lord and emptied of the old nature that is set on its old ways and ambitions (Ephesians 5:18). Peter and the other disciples were filled with the Spirit on the day of Pentecost (Acts 2:4). But later when warned and threatened by the Jewish leaders not to speak and teach in Jesus' name, the disciples prayed, and Peter and the others were filled again with the Spirit and power (Acts 4:8; 4:31). The power of the Spirit is necessary for the preacher to speak boldly and effectively the word of God.

His Early Years

After his conversion Paul, filled with the Spirit, began to preach in the synagogues in Damascus with forthrightness and boldness that Jesus is the Son of God. The people were astounded that the man who was leading in the persecution of Christians was proclaiming Christ with great power. He grew more and more powerful with effectiveness in the days following, baffling the Jews and proving that Jesus is the Messiah, the Christ. But the unbelieving Jews and their leaders conspired to kill him, and the disciples helped him to escape in a basket over the city walls.

He fled to Jerusalem and tried to join the disciples there, but they were afraid of him. However, Barnabas took him to the apostles and told them how Paul met the Lord on the road to Damascus and spoken to him, and how he preached fearlessly in the name of Christ in the city. He was accepted by the disciples and moved freely around the city, preaching boldly in the name of the Lord. He talked and debated with the Grecian Jews, but though some of them believed the word of the Lord, most of them rejected the message and planned to kill him. The disciples thought it best to take him to Caesarea and then later to his home in Tarsus. Thus Paul began his ministry with great boldness, power, and effectiveness, but with opposition to him and his message (Acts 9:26-30). However, he remained steadfast and committed to his commission from God to carry his name to the people of Israel and the Gentiles as the Lord guided him.

In Antioch of Pisidia

After some years, including three years in seclusion in Arabia, Barnabas brought Paul to Antioch in Syria where they served with other prophets and teachers. The Holy Spirit called them to a missionary journey to Asia Minor, where they began proclaiming the word of God first in Jewish synagogues. In Antioch of Pisidia they were called on to speak a word of encouragement. Paul preached the gospel and made an appeal to receive Jesus as Messiah, the Savior, warning them against rejection as some prophets predicted might happen. Many were interested and asked him to speak further about the matter the next week. Many of the Jews and God-fearing Gentiles followed Paul and Barnabas who urged them to continue in the grace of God (Acts 13:42-43). But some of the Jewish leaders saw the large crowds from the city interested in and responding to the word of God and were jealous, speaking abusively against them. Paul and Barnabas responded, saying boldly, "We had to speak the word of God to you first. Since you rejected it and do not consider yourselves worthy of eternal life, we now turn to the Gentiles. For this is what the Lord has commanded us" (Acts 13:46-47; Isaiah 49:6).

When the Gentiles heard this message, they were glad, honoring the word of God and receiving eternal life. The word of God spread throughout the region, and a few women of high standing and some leading men received the word. Again, the Jewish leaders stirred up opposition and persecuted them. So they left for Iconium, but the new disciples were filled with joy and the Holy Spirit (Acts 13:48-52).

This pattern continued throughout western Asia Minor, with some Jews and proselytes accepting Paul's message of the gospel, but with others rejecting it and stirring up opposition. Many Gentiles then accepted the message of Christ. Though Paul continued to enter synagogues first to proclaim the word of God, he turned more and more to the Gentiles. He continued to preach the gospel throughout the area, especially Iconium, Lystra, and Derbe. On his return to Antioch of Syria, he encouraged and strengthened the disciples to remain true to the faith, appointing elders in the churches and committing the believers to the Lord (Acts 14:1-21).

At the Council in Jerusalem

When Paul and Barnabas returned to Antioch, they gathered the church and reported on the great things that God had done in opening the door of faith to the Gentiles. Some men came from Judea teaching the brethren that unless they are circumcised according to the law of Moses, they cannot be saved. Paul and Barnabas had a sharp disagreement about this matter and debated with them. So the church sent them and others to Jerusalem to discuss this question with apostles and elders. When they arrived, they were welcomed by the church and the leaders and reported everything that God had done through them, especially the conversion of the Gentiles, which made the brothers glad (Acts 15:1-4).

The church council was called to resolve this problem. Peter spoke how God had appeared to him and showed him how the Gentiles should be privileged to hear the gospel and were accepted even as the Jews, giving them the Holy Spirit also. For there is no distinction between them; both are saved by the grace of the Lord Jesus. Paul and Barnabas then spoke of the miraculous signs and wonders that God had done among the Gentiles through them. James, the chief spokesman of the council, spoke up saying that the prophets were in agreement, and they should not make it more difficult for the Gentiles who were turning to the Lord. So a letter was sent with Paul and Barnabas who were accompanied by Judas and Silas confirming this great truth. The Gentiles should not be burdened with anything beyond the requirements of abstaining from food offered to idols, from sexual immorality, from meat of strangled animals, and from blood (Acts 15:12-29).

In Athens

After returning to Antioch they delivered the letter, and the disciples were glad for the encouraging report. Paul then said to Barnabas that they ought to visit the cities where they preached the word and see how they were doing. Over a dispute about taking Mark again, who left them on the first journey, Paul took Silas and delivered the decisions of the council while Barnabas took Mark to Cyprus. The churches in Asia Minor were strengthened and grew daily in large numbers. Paul and Silas were guided by the Holy Spirit to Macedonia and were effective in spreading the gospel. They were able to reach many among the Jews and Gentiles in Philippi, Thessalonica, and Berea, explaining and proving that Christ had to suffer and rise from the dead and that Jesus is truly the Christ. But again the unbelieving Jews stirred up opposition; so Paul went on to Athens (Acts 15:30-17:15).

While waiting for Silas and Timothy, Paul was greatly distressed about the idolatry of the people. He reasoned with the Jews and God-fearing Gentiles in the synagogues and in the market places each day. When a group of Epicurean and Stoic philosophers began to dispute with him regarding Jesus and the resurrection, they gave him opportunity to speak at the Areopagus. There he delivered his message around the altar TO AN UNKNOWN GOD, based on the subject "The unknown God has made himself known." When he concluded by making an appeal to repent based on the resurrection of Jesus from the dead, some sneered but others wanted to hear more on the subject. A few men became followers and believed, including Dionysius, a member of the Aeropagus, and a woman named Damaris and some others (Acts 17:22-34). The response was small in number since the audience had no background of the Old Testament and of the Christian faith. However, in the years following, the church grew in numbers and strength because of the seed that was sown by Paul proclaiming the word of God by the Spirit of God. The records of the history of the early church indicate the growth of the church in Athens and surrounding areas.

In Miletus

After considerable success in the region of Achaia, though under considerable hardships, Paul returned to Syria. On his third missionary journey, he traveled throughout the regions of Galatia and Phrygia strengthening the disciples and winning many to Christ, especially in the strategic city of Ephesus, which served as a base to reach the surrounding areas of western Asia Minor. He set out for Macedonia and other territories of Greece proclaiming the word of God with considerable success. Then he decided to return to Jerusalem and was in a hurry to reach there by the day of Pentecost. So he sent for the elders of the church at Ephesus to meet him in Miletus. There he delivered the pastoral message to the faithful shepherds of the church of God. He reminded them of the example he set when he served with them, challenging them to watch over the flock that the Holy Spirit made them overseers and warning them of the dangers ahead from men who would distort the truth and scatter the flock. The message was received gracefully but with sadness and grief that they would not see him again. He knelt down with them and prayed for them. They wept, embraced him, and accompanied him to the ship. Great love was manifested during the brief visit. In the years following, the churches in Ephesus and surrounding areas grew in number and size, including the seven churches discussed in the book of Revelation. These churches became centers of evangelistic outreach in the decades following under the leadership of the churches and their leaders in western Asia Minor (Acts 20:13-38; Revelation 2-3).

In Jerusalem

Paul was received warmly in Jerusalem by James, the apostles, and many of the elders, and he reported in detail what the Lord had done through his ministry among the Gentiles. But many Jews were concerned about the law of Moses and accused him of not requiring the Gentiles to be circumcised and to keep the Jewish customs. Trying to appease them, he was asked to take a vow to show that he was living in obedience to the law. But an uproar occurred when some of the Jews accused him of taking a Gentile into the temple area and defiling the holy place. The Roman troops saved him from being killed and took him to their barracks. He was allowed to speak and gave a strong testimony in his defense. When he concluded his message saying that the Lord had sent him to testify before the Gentiles, the crowd raised their voices wanting to execute him. The Roman commander protected him when he discovered that he was a Roman citizen. Paul manifested faith in the Lord's ability to deliver him and protect him to fulfill his calling to spread the gospel especially to the Gentiles (Acts 21:40-22:29).

Paul addressed an antagonistic audience who was prejudiced and unbelieving. But by the grace of God he was protected in a fearful situation showing courage, but with little response to the power of the gospel. But the Lord stood by him, saying, "Take courage! As you have testified about me in Jerusalem, so you must also testify in Rome" (Acts 23:11).

In Caesarea

Paul was sent to Caesarea under Roman guard to protect him from a plot to kill him. The Roman governor Felix was to hear the charges against him by the Jewish leaders who claimed that he was a troublemaker, stirring up riots against the Jews all over the world, and a ringleader of the sect of Nazarenes. The Roman world was taking notice of the message of the Christian faith through the apostle Paul. He was again allowed to speak in his defense and testify that he worshiped the God of their fathers, believing in everything written in the law and the prophets. He then charged that the real reason he was on trial was for the matter concerning the resurrection from the dead (Acts 24:1-21).

He was held in prison for two years until Festus became governor. He was given the opportunity to speak in his defense before King Agrippa in an assembly of ranking officials and leading men of the city. He again gave his testimony to an audience which was not so antagonistic as the one in Jerusalem, but was more inquisitive and fair since Paul was a Roman citizen. He wisely concluded his message by claiming that what Moses had said would happen: the Christ would suffer and rise from the dead and that light would be proclaimed to his own people and also to the Gentiles. Festus responded by saying, "You are out of your mind, Paul!...Your great learning is driving you insane" (Acts 26:24). Therefore, Paul appealed to King Agrippa who he said believed the prophets. The king responded by saying to Paul, "Do you think that in such a short time you can persuade me to be a Christian?" (Acts 26:28). Therefore Paul was effective in convincing them of some of the claims of Christ and the need of trusting in him. The king told Festus that he did not deserve death or imprisonment, but since he appealed to Caesar he could not be set free. Thus Paul was declared innocent of the charges. His defense was persuasive and provided him an opportunity to travel to Rome at government expense where the Lord said he would bear witness also (Acts 26:30-32).

In Rome

As in all of his journeys, the Lord guarded Paul along the way and empowered him to accomplish great things. After a hazardous trip by ship, he was again led by the Lord and assured that he would arrive safely in spite of a shipwreck. An angel of the Lord reminded him that he must stand trial before Caesar's court. God graciously saved all aboard ship. He told the people to take courage for " I have faith in God" that he will save us all (Acts 27:21-26).

When he arrived at Puteoli south of Rome, some of the brethren met him, and he gave thanks to God and was encouraged. He reported that he had done nothing against the Jewish people or against their customs. The Roman leaders wanted to release him since he was not guilty of any crimes worthy of death, but he had appealed to Caesar. When he arrived in Rome, a large group of people gathered to hear him. From morning to evening he explained matters regarding the truth about the kingdom of God. He persuaded them to believe in Christ as prophesied in the law of Moses and the prophets. Some agreed with him and were persuaded to accept Jesus as the Christ, but others refused. Paul gave this parting word:

> The Holy Spirit spoke the truth to your forefathers when he said through Isaiah the prophet: 'Go to this people and say, You will be ever hearing but never understanding; you will be ever seeing but never perceiving' (Isaiah 6:9; Acts 28:25-26).

Moreover, he went on to say that God's salvation has been sent to the Gentiles who will listen.

For two full years Paul welcomed all who came to his rented house. He was always guarded by a Roman soldier. He proclaimed the kingdom of God boldly without any interference and taught about the Lord Jesus Christ (Acts 28:30-31). Thus from the beginning of his public ministry, Paul preached the word of God in the power of the Spirit with great effectiveness. In his thirty-five year ministry, he reached people for Christ in much of the Roman world with the gospel in his lifetime through preaching, teaching, establishing churches, ordaining ministers, defending the faith, and writing letters, many of which were preserved as inspired Scriptures. He took the message first to the Jews, and when their leaders rejected the message, he turned to the Gentiles, many of these receiving Christ as Savior and Lord. His conversion to the Lord and his calling to reach the world for Christ, especially the Gentiles, was so crucial that they are recorded three times in the book of Acts by Luke. He was set for the defense of the gospel, stressing the vital need of receiving Christ by faith for salvation (Philippians 1:15-19; 27-30). Paul accomplished his ministry as recorded in Scripture in his Christian witness to the world through the proclamation of the gospel, setting an example for churches and leaders.

CHAPTER VIII

HIS INSTRUCTIONS ON PREACHING

In his letters Paul had much to say about preaching, especially in his letters to the Romans and Corinthians. The Greek words used most often for proclaiming the word of God are preaching (*kerygma*), the message preached, preacher (*kerux*), the herald, and to preach (*kerussein*), the action of preaching. The other word used often is to preach the gospel (*euangelizesthai*) that means to proclaim the good news or evangelize. It comes from the basic word meaning gospel (*euangelion*) or good news derived from good (*eu*) and news or message (*angelos*). The messenger or preacher, also (*angelos*), is the one who announces the good news. These are the primary words, but the following words previously indicated in chapter three are also used: to speak (*lalein*), to exhort (*parakalein*), to witness (*marturein*), to prophesy (*propheteuein*), and to teach (*didaskein*). His use of all of these expressions contribute to his instruction on the subject of preaching.

Romans

Paul's teaching on preaching in the letter to the Romans is centered primarily on the content of preaching based on the gospel and on the scope of preaching which includes the Gentiles. He opened his letter to the Romans by stating his calling as an apostle set apart for the gospel as follows:

> Paul, a servant of Christ Jesus, called to be an apostle and set apart for the gospel of God—the gospel he promised beforehand through his prophets in the Holy Scriptures regarding his Son, who as to his human nature was a descendant of David, who through the Spirit of holiness was declared with power to be the Son of God by his resurrection from the dead: Jesus Christ our Lord. Through him and for his name's sake, we received grace and apostleship to call people from among all the Gentiles to the obedience that comes from faith (Romans 1:1-5).

He described here what the prophets promised beforehand in the Holy Scriptures regarding the human nature of Jesus Christ and his divine nature by the Holy Spirit. He was declared to be the Son of God with power by his resurrection from the dead. Through him, Paul received apostleship to call the Gentiles to obedience to the faith.

He reminded the Roman Christians that he was obligated to preach the gospel to them in Rome. The theme of the letter is then stated as follows:

> I am not ashamed of the gospel, because it is the power of God for the salvation of everyone who believes: first for the Jew, then for the Gentile. For in the gospel a righteousness from God is revealed, a righteousness that is by faith from first to

last, just as it is written: 'The righteous will live by faith' (Habakkuk 2:4; Romans 1:16-17).

The gospel is the power of God for salvation of everyone who believes. In the gospel God's righteousness is revealed, for the righteous ones will live by faith.

Later in the letter he declared that Abraham, the father of the faithful, was credited with righteousness through his faith as are all people who believe in Christ, writing:

> Yet he did not waver through unbelief regarding the promise of God, but was strengthened in his faith and gave glory to God, being fully persuaded that God had power to do what he had promised. This is why 'it was credited to him as righteousness.' The words 'it was credited to him' were written not for him alone, but also for us, to whom God will credit righteousness—for us who believe in him who raised Jesus our Lord from the dead. He was delivered over to death for our sins and was raised to life for our justification (Romans 4:20-25).

Thus believers are justified through faith and have peace with God through the Lord Jesus Christ.

At the close of this doctrinal section of the letter, he again summarized his views of the gospel regarding justification by faith as follows:

> What, then, shall we say in response to this? If God is for us, who can be against us? He who did not spare his own Son, but gave him up for us all—how will he not also, along with him, graciously give us all things? Who will bring any charge against those whom God has chosen? It is God who justifies. Who is he that condemns? Christ Jesus, who died—more than that, who was raised to life—is at the right hand of God and also is interceding for us (Romans 8:31-34).

The message of faith, that is the word of faith, which he was preaching, is as follows:

> But what does it say? 'The word is near you; it is in your mouth and in your heart,' that is, the word of faith we are proclaiming: That if you confess with your mouth, 'Jesus is Lord,' and believe in your heart that God raised him from the dead, you will be saved. For it is with your heart that you believe and are justified, and it is with your mouth that you confess and are saved. As the Scripture says, 'Anyone who trusts in him will never be put to shame.' For there is no difference between Jew and Gentile—the same Lord is Lord of all and richly blesses all who call on him, for, 'Everyone who calls on the name of the Lord will be saved.' How, then, can they call on the one they have not believed in? And how can they believe in the one whom they have not heard? And how can they hear without someone preaching to them? And how can they preach unless they are sent? As it is written, 'How beautiful are the feet of those who bring good news!' (Romans 10:8-15).

He explained that the response needed to be saved is faith in the resurrected Christ, calling on him as Lord and confessing with the mouth as Savior. Because people will not call on one whom they have never heard about, God calls on the preachers he sends to proclaim the gospel, the good news, to them.

In the center section of the letter, Paul stated that only a remnant of the Jews accepted the Lord, so the Gentiles were offered salvation and received into the family of God. He reminded the Romans that he was an apostle to the Gentiles and magnified his ministry in the hope that he might provoke his own people to be saved (Romans 11:13-14). This was so important to them and the world at that time. He was a minister of Jesus Christ to the Gentiles through the grace God gave him. His duty was to preach the gospel of God so that his offering of them to God may be acceptable and sanctified by the Holy Spirit. Thus he indicated his dedication and determination to do what God called him to do (Roman 15:15-16). He preached the gospel from Jerusalem to Illyricum, the frontier province of the Grecian borders. His ambition was to preach the gospel where Christ was not known. He planned to visit Rome and Spain also, reaching much of the known world (Romans 15:17-24).

In his closing words Paul warned those who cause divisions and obstacles contrary to what he taught and they learned. They were not serving the Lord, but by smooth talk and flattery deceived naive people. He closed with this benediction:

> Now to him who is able to establish you by my gospel and the proclamation of Jesus Christ, according to the revelation of the mystery hidden for long ages past, but now revealed and made known through the prophetic writings by the command of the eternal God, so that all nations might believe and obey him—to the only wise God be glory forever through Jesus Christ! Amen (Roman 16:25-27).

He reminded them that God is able to establish them by his gospel and the proclamation (*kerygma*) of Jesus Christ according to the revelation, once a hidden mystery, but now made known through the prophetic writings by God's command that all nations might believe and obey him.

In his letter to the Romans, Paul emphasized that people are justified by grace through faith by the gospel proclaimed to Jews and Gentiles alike. The gospel is the good news of Christ's death for sin and sinners, saving them from sin and death and giving them eternal life. Everyone must accept the resurrected Christ as Savior and Lord. The good news must be proclaimed as exemplified by Paul to ministers, Christians, and churches.

Corinthians

In his letters to the Corinthians, Paul had much to say about preaching and preaching the gospel, that is evangelistic preaching. In his opening words he thanked God for the grace given to them in speaking and knowledge, which were particular gifts confirmed in his testimony about Christ (1 Corinthians 1:4-9). He furthermore acknowledged that Christ had commissioned him to preach the gospel (*euangelizesthai*), not with words of human wisdom, lest the cross of Christ should be made ineffective (1 Corinthians 1:17). He then stressed the importance of the wisdom and power of the cross, writing:

> For the message of the cross is foolishness to those who are perishing, but to us who are being saved it is the power of God. For it is written: 'I will destroy the wisdom of the wise; the intelligence of the intelligent I will frustrate.' Where is the wise man? Where is the scholar? Where is the philosopher of this age? Has not God made foolish the wisdom of the world? For since in the wisdom of God the world through its wisdom did not know him, God was pleased through the foolishness of what was preached to save those who believe. Jews demand miraculous signs and Greeks look for wisdom, but we preach Christ crucified: a stumbling block to Jews and foolishness to Gentiles, but to those whom God has called, both Jews and Greeks, Christ the power of God and the wisdom of God. For the foolishness of God is wiser than man's wisdom, and the weakness of God is stronger than man's strength (1 Corinthians 1:18-25).

For God had chosen through the foolishness of preaching, as far as the world is concerned, to save those who believe in the message preached (*kerygma*). To those who believe, whether Jews or Greeks, Christ crucified is the power of God and the wisdom of God. The message preached is through the power of God, not through enticing words of man's wisdom.

Moreover, he emphasized the following and wrote:

> When I came to you, brothers, I did not come with eloquence or superior wisdom as I proclaimed to you the testimony about God. For I resolved to know nothing while I was with you except Jesus Christ and him crucified. I came to you in weakness and fear, and with much trembling. My message and my preaching were not with wise and persuasive words, but with a demonstration of the Spirit's power, so that your faith might not rest on men's wisdom, but on God's power. We do, however, speak a message of wisdom among the mature, but not the wisdom of this age or of the rulers of this age, who are coming to nothing. No, we speak of God's secret wisdom, a wisdom that has been hidden and that God destined for our glory before time began. None of the rulers of this age understood it, for if they had, they would not have crucified the Lord of glory (1 Corinthians 2:1-8).

Paul determined to preach the testimony of God not with eloquence and wisdom with persuasive words, but in fact in weakness and fear and in demonstration of the Spirit and of power, so that their faith would not stand in the wisdom of man, but in the power of God. The Spirit of God is the one who searches men's hearts. Paul said; "But God has revealed it to us by his Spirit," writing:

> The Spirit searches all things, even the deep things of God. For who among men knows the thoughts of a man except the man's spirit within him? In the same

way no one knows the thoughts of God except the Spirit of God. We have not received the spirit of the world but the Spirit who is from God, that we may understand what God has freely given us. This is what we speak, not in words taught us by human wisdom but in words taught by the Spirit, expressing spiritual truths in spiritual words. The man without the Spirit does not accept the things from the Spirit of God, for they are foolishness to him, and he cannot understand them, because they are spiritually discerned. The spiritual man makes judgments about all things, but he himself is not subject to any man's judgment. 'For who has known the mind of the Lord that he may instruct him?' But we have the mind of Christ (1 Corinthians 2:10-16).

Thus, the Spirit of God is the teacher and helps people to understand spiritual truths. Therefore, the preacher is dependent upon the Spirit to speak through him to convince them to accept Christ.

Paul warns apostles and preachers not to deceive themselves and boast of their accomplishments, which really come through Christ. They are servants of Christ and entrusted with the mysteries of God. It is required of them to prove themselves faithful of their trust (1 Corinthians 3:18-4:2). But the Lord has commanded that those who preach the gospel should receive their living from the ministry of proclaiming the gospel. But he was not writing them in hope of receiving things for himself. When he preached the word, he was compelled to do it by the Lord. But he wrote to them this appeal:

> In the same way, the Lord has commanded that those that preach the gospel should receive their living from the gospel. But I have not used any of these rights. And I am not writing this in hope that you will do such things for me. I would rather die than have anyone deprive me of this boast. Yet when I preach the gospel, I cannot boast, for I am compelled to preach. Woe to me if I do not preach the gospel! If I preach voluntarily, I have a reward; if not voluntarily, I am simply discharging the trust committed to me. What then is my reward? Just this: that in preaching the gospel I may offer it free of charge, and so not make use of my rights in preaching it (1 Corinthians 9:14-18).

He strove to become all things to all men that he might win those who were under the law and not under the law. He kept his body under subjection so that after he had preached the word of God, he would not be disqualified. Instead he would receive the incorruptible crown of life as the runner who runs the race and receives the prize (1 Corinthians 9:24-27).

Not only do men proclaim the Lord's death but also the ordinance of the Lord's Supper proclaims this message. He wrote:

> For I received of the Lord what I also passed on to you. The Lord Jesus, on the night he was betrayed, took bread, and when he had given thanks, he broke it and said, 'This is my body, which is for you; do this in remembrance of me.' In the same way, after supper he took the cup, saying, 'This cup is the new covenant in my blood; do this, whenever you drink it, in remembrance of me.' For whenever

you eat this bread and drink this cup, you proclaim the Lord's death until he comes (1 Corinthians 11:23-26).

When Christians partake of the bread and the cup, they proclaim (*kataggellete*) the death the Lord until he comes again. In effect they proclaim the gospel in participating in the Lord's Supper. This is a word which is related to evangelize (*euangelizesthai*) and means to declare openly, to proclaim, or to preach the gospel. In effect, baptism also proclaims the gospel; the death, burial, and resurrection of Christ as he wrote to the Romans (Romans 6:3-4).

Paul wrote extensively about spiritual gifts. He indicated that there are different kinds of spiritual gifts for different kinds of service, but the same God working through these gifts in men as God determines. He stated:

> Now to each one the manifestation of the Spirit is given for the common good. To one there is given through the Spirit the message of wisdom, to another the message of knowledge by means of the same Spirit, to another faith by the same Spirit, to another gifts of healing by that one Spirit, to another miraculous powers, to another prophecy, to another distinguishing between spirits, to another speaking in different kinds of tongues, and to still another the interpretation of tongues. All these are the work of one and the same Spirit, and he gives gifts to each one, just as he determines (1 Corinthians 12:7-11).

Four of the gifts have to do with speaking, namely, give the message of wisdom, give the message of knowledge, prophesying, and speaking in tongues, or different kinds of languages. All these gifts work together by the same Spirit who gives to each as he determines.

In the church, which is the body of Christ, each Christian has his part in its ministry. Paul wrote to these gifted Corinthians, saying:

> Now you are the body of Christ, and each one of you is a part of it. And in the church God has appointed first of all apostles, second prophets, third teachers, then workers of miracles, also those having gifts of healing, those able to help others, those with gifts of administration, and those speaking in different kinds of tongues (1 Corinthians 12:27-28).

In this same letter Paul declared the clearest presentation of the very core of the gospel (*euangelion*) that he preached (*euangelizesthai*) unto them, writing:

> Now, brothers, I want to remind you of the gospel I preached to you, which you received and on which you have taken your stand. By this gospel you are saved, if you hold firmly to the word I preached to you. Otherwise, you have believed in vain. For what I received I passed on to you as of first importance: that Christ died for our sins according to the Scriptures, that he was buried, that he was raised on the third day according to the Scriptures, and that he appeared to Peter, and then to the Twelve. After that, he appeared to more than five hundred of the brothers at the same time, most of whom are still living, though some have fallen

asleep. Then he appeared to James, then to all the apostles, and last of all he appeared to me also, as to one abnormally born (1 Corinthians 15:1-8).

As indicated in the chapter on doctrine, the death, burial, and resurrection of Christ according to the Scriptures is the central truth of the gospel. Some Old Testament passages that he referred to indicating his death could be Isaiah 53 and his resurrection Psalm 16:8-11, which he quoted in his message to the people of Antioch of Pisidia. He believed that he was the least of the apostles because he persecuted the church of God. Nevertheless, he worked harder than all of them by the grace of God, which was only possible because of this grace of God that was in him. Either way whether it was by them or him, this gospel was preached and this is what the Corinthians believed.

Paul followed this presentation of the gospel with great emphasis on the fact of the resurrection of the dead. He concluded that Christ who he proclaimed was raised from the dead, the first of those resurrected who had fallen asleep in death. This is the hope of all believers, for death is swallowed up in victory at the second coming of Christ when they are resurrected from the dead as Christ rose from the dead (1 Corinthians 15:12-20; 54-56).

In his second letter to the Corinthians, Paul dealt with some concerns about them, corrected some misunderstandings, enlarged on some great truths, defended his ministry, and offered some warnings. He reminded them that God is faithful, his message is true, and Jesus Christ, the Son of God, was preached to them by him, Silas, and Timothy (2 Corinthians 1:18-19). When he went to Troas, he preached the gospel and found a door opened to him to the Greek world. He thanked God who always led him to triumph in Christ. He did not peddle the word of God for profit, but in Christ he spoke the word before God with sincerity as one sent by God (2 Corinthians 2:12-17). He spoke of the new covenant in Christ with boldness and plainness of speech (2 Corinthians 3:6-12). They did not preach themselves but Jesus Christ as Lord and themselves as servants for Jesus' sake (2 Corinthians 4:5).

Paul later made an appeal for a ministry of reconciliation. Everyone must appear before the judgment seat of Christ and receive what is due him for the things done in the body, whether good or bad (2 Corinthians 5:10). Based on this fact and the love of Christ, he wrote:

> For Christ's love compels us, because we are convinced that one died for all, and therefore all died. And he died for all, that those who live should no longer live for themselves but for him who died for them and was raised again. So from now on we regard no one from a worldly point of view. Though we once regarded Christ in this way, we do so no longer. Therefore, if anyone is in Christ, he is a new creation; the old has gone, the new has come! All this is from God, who reconciled us to himself through Christ and gave us the ministry of reconciliation: that God was reconciling the world to himself in Christ not counting men's sins against them. And he has committed to us the message of reconciliation. We are therefore Christ's ambassadors, as though God were making his appeal through us. We implore you on Christ's behalf: Be reconciled to God. God made him who

had no sin to be sin for us, so that in him we might become the righteousness of God. As God's fellow workers we urge you not to receive God's grace in vain. For he says, 'In the time of my favor I heard you, and in the day of salvation I helped you.' I tell you, now is the time of God's favor, now is day of salvation (2 Corinthians 5:14-6:2).

Christians as God's ambassadors have committed unto them the message of reconciliation, and God makes this appeal to people through them on Christ's behalf, saying, "Be reconciled to God." Therefore, as God's fellow workers, he urges them not to receive the grace of God in vain, but receive God's grace, for "now is the time of God's favor, now is the day of salvation."

Paul expressed concern for the Corinthian Christians, whom he had served and protected. For other men had come and preached another Jesus whom he had not preached, or received a different spirit from the one they had not received, or a different gospel which they had not accepted. He was not inferior in knowledge and knew what he was talking about. He made this perfectly clear to them (2 Corinthians 11:1-6). In fact he claimed that Christ was speaking through him regarding these matters (2 Corinthians 13:2-3).

Galatians

Paul dealt with the same problem in his letter to the Galatians. He contended:

I am astonished that you are so quickly deserting the one who called you by the grace of Christ and are turning to a different gospel—which is really no gospel at all. Evidently some people are throwing you into confusion and trying to pervert the gospel of Christ. But even if we or an angel from heaven should preach a gospel other than the one we preached to you, let him be eternally condemned! As we have already said, so now I say again: If anybody is preaching to you a gospel other than what you accepted, let him be eternally condemned (Galatians 1:6-9)!

He was severe with them, and especially with those who were preaching another gospel or perverting the gospel of Christ. In his defense, he further argued:

Am I now trying to win approval of men, or of God? Or am I trying to please men? If I were still trying to please men, I would not be a servant of Christ. I want you to know, brothers, that the gospel I preached is not something that man made up. I did not receive it from any man, nor was I taught it; rather, I received it by revelation from Jesus Christ (Galatians 1:10-12).

He went on to describe his former life and his persecution of the church before he met the Lord and his call by God, writing:

For you have heard of my previous way of life in Judaism, how intensely I persecuted the church of God and tried to destroy it. I was advancing in Judaism beyond many Jews of my own age and was extremely zealous for the traditions of my fathers. But when God, who set me apart from birth and called me by his grace, was pleased to reveal his Son in me so that I might preach him among the Gentiles, I did not consult man (Galatians 1:13-16).

He did not consult the apostles or any other men, but went into the desert for three years to consider his calling. Then he went to the apostles and the other leaders in Jerusalem to discuss the matter concerning his call to preach the gospel to the Gentiles. They accepted him and his ministry as described by Luke in the book of Acts (Acts 9:22-27; Galatians 1:11-2:5).

He went on to defend the faith before the Galatians who were being deceived by the Judaizers, and were leading them astray, saying the Gentiles had to keep the customs of the Jewish laws. This was a crucial issue with the early church, and thus his major concern and emphasis in his preaching and correspondence to the Galatian Christians (Galatians 3:1-14).

Ephesians

In his letter to the Ephesians, Paul emphasized the mystery of Christ, which had not been known previously. But it was at this time revealed by the holy prophets and apostles that through the gospel the Gentiles became heirs with Israel in one body, shared together in the promise in Jesus Christ (Ephesians 3:1-6). He declared:

> I became a servant of this gospel by the gift of God's grace given me through the working of his power. Although I am the less than the least of all God's people, this grace was given me: to preach to the Gentiles the unsearchable riches of Christ, and to make plain to everyone the administration of this mystery, which for ages past was kept hidden in God, who created all things. His intent was that now, through the church, the manifold wisdom of God should be known to the rulers and authorities in the heavenly realms, according to his eternal purpose which he which he accomplished in Christ Jesus our Lord. In him and through faith in him we may approach God with freedom and confidence (Ephesians 3:7-12).

God's intent then through the church was to make known the mystery of the unsearchable riches of Christ and to preach this to the Gentiles. In order to do this, Christ gave to the church gifted messengers. Paul declared:

> It was he who gave some to be apostles, some to be prophets, some to be evangelists, and some to be pastors and teachers, to prepare God's people for works of service, so that the body of Christ may be built up until we all reach unity in the of faith and in the knowledge of the Son of God and become mature, attaining to the whole measure of the fullness of Christ (Ephesians 4:11-13).

Therefore, Christians would no longer be tossed about by every wind of doctrine by the cunning and craftiness through deceitful schemes, but rather to speak the truth in love. Thus, they would grow together in Christ, who is the head of the church (Ephesians 4:14-16).

To a matter related to preaching, Paul warns Gentile Christians to remember what they had been taught, namely, to put off the nature of the old life corrupted by evil desires and lying, but rather to speak truthfully to their neighbors. They were not to let unwholesome talk to come out of their mouths, but only what is helpful for edifying others and for their benefit (Ephesians 4:20-29). He summarized this by writing:

> And do not grieve the Holy Spirit of God, with whom you were sealed for the day of redemption. Get rid of all bitterness, rage and anger, brawling and slander, along with every form of malice. Be kind and compassionate to one another, forgiving each other, just as in Christ God forgave you. Be imitators of God, therefore, as dearly loved children and live a life of love, just as Christ loved us and gave himself up for us as a fragrant offering and sacrifice to God (Ephesians 4:30-32; 5:1-2).

Especially important is the exhortation to be kind and compassionate and forgiving as God forgives us in Christ. Christians were to make the most of every opportunity and understand what is the will of God. They were not to be drunk with wine, but to be filled with the Spirit, speaking to one another with psalms, hymns, and spiritual songs, singing from their hearts to the Lord and giving thanks to God the Father for everything in Jesus name (Ephesians 5:15-20). Paul emphasized speaking for Christ and making known the word of God. He requested prayer for him that whenever he spoke, the words would be given to him and that he would make known the gospel boldly and fearlessly as he should as an ambassador for Christ (Ephesians 6:19-20).

Philippians

In his letter to the Philippians, Paul, writing from a Roman prison, said that the troubles he was having really served to advance the gospel. As a result of this, many of the palace guard and other staff members trusted in Christ. In fact his example encouraged many other Christians to speak the word of God more courageously and fearlessly (Philippians 1:12-14). He wrote this contrast:

> It is true that some preach Christ out of envy and rivalry, but others out of goodwill. The latter do so in love, knowing that I am put here for the defense of the gospel. The former preach Christ out of selfish ambition, not sincerely, supposing that they can stir up trouble for me while I am in chains. But what does it matter? The important thing is that in every way, whether from false motives or true, Christ is preached. And because of this I rejoice (Philippians 1:15-18).

Furthermore, he said that he would continue to rejoice, knowing that through their prayers and the help of the Spirit of Jesus Christ that the things happening to him would turn out for his eventual deliverance. Moreover, he would have sufficient courage so that Christ would be exalted in his body, whether by life or by death (Philippians 1:19-20). To be with Christ is far better, but for the present time, it was more needful for them that he remain in the body (Philippians 1:21-26). So he pressed on to take hold for what the Lord had for him to do, namely, to strive for prize of the high calling of God in Christ Jesus (Philippians 3:12-14).

Colossians

In his letter to the Colossian people, Paul dealt with problems regarding the proclamation of the word of God. Christians were being led astray from the truth of the gospel as those in the Galatian and Ephesian churches. He reminded them of their past and present conditions, writing:

> Once you were alienated from God and were enemies in your minds because of your evil behavior. But now he has reconciled you by Christ's physical body through death to present you holy in his sight, without blemish and free from accusation—if you continue in your faith, established and firm, not moved from the hope held out in the gospel. This is the gospel that you heard and that has been proclaimed to every creature under heaven, and of which I, Paul, have become a servant (Colossians 1:21-23).

They had the gospel proclaimed to them as to every person under heaven, including the Gentiles. Paul was a servant, commissioned by God to present the word of God in its fullness. For God had made Jesus Christ known among all the people the glorious riches of this mystery, that is, Christ in you, the hope of glory (Colossians 1:25-27).

Paul worked hard for the church at Colossae in behalf of Christ, declaring:

> We proclaim him, admonishing and teaching everyone with all wisdom, so that we may present everyone perfect in Christ. To this end I labor, struggling with all his energy, which so powerfully works in me (Colossians 1:28-29).

He continually gave credit to Christ who worked in him powerfully to accomplish his works.

He also requested prayer for himself, as he did from the Ephesians, that God would open a door of opportunity to proclaim the mystery of Christ clearly as he should. He implored them to let their speech be full of grace and seasoned with salt, that is winsomeness, so that they may know how to answer everyone clearly (Colossians 4:2-6).

Thessalonians

Two of Paul's earliest letters were first and second Thessalonians, written to the church in the Greek city of Thessalonica. Like the last of his three pastoral letters, they refer to most of the significant words used to express the proclamation of the word of God: to preach (*kerussein*) or proclaim the gospel most often, but also to speak, to exhort, to witness, to prophesy, and to teach the word. This indicates that from the beginning of his ministry to the end of it, Paul emphasized the strategic importance of preaching to reach the world for Christ.

In his first letter to the Thessalonians, he wrote this important word regarding preaching, which was also discussed in the chapter on his power and effectiveness:

> For we know, brothers loved by God, that he has chosen you, because our gospel came to you not simply with words, but also with power, with the Holy Spirit and with deep conviction. You know how we lived among you for your sake (1 Thessalonians 1:4-5).

These ways that the gospel is presented are absolutely essential if it is effective in reaching people for Christ: by the word of the gospel, by power, by the Holy Spirit, by deep conviction, and by living for him. This was the way the word of God spread in Macedonia and Achaia, including Thessalonica and everywhere their faith toward God was proclaimed. They turned from idols to serve the living God and to wait for his Son from heaven, whom he raised from the dead (I Thessalonians 1:8-10).

Paul dared to preach the gospel to the Greeks with conviction in spite of strong opposition, but his motive was pure. He could write:

> For the appeal we make does not spring from error or impure motives, nor are we trying to trick you. On the contrary, we speak as men approved by God to be entrusted with the gospel. We are not trying to please men but God, who tests our hearts. You know we never used flattery, nor did we put on a mask to cover up greed—God is our witness. We are not looking for praise from men, not from you or anyone else (1 Thessalonians 2:3-6).

He thanked God continually because they received the word of God, which they heard from him in sincerity, not as the word of men, but as it actually was, the word of God, at work in them that believe (1 Thessalonians 2:13).

In his letter he urged them to love each other and to be holy, avoiding sexual immorality, for this is God's will. Moreover, they were to live in hope of Christ's coming, for some Christians were grieving as men over the death of loved ones who had no hope. He made this appeal:

> Brothers, we do not want you to be ignorant about those who fall asleep, or to grieve like the rest of men, who have no hope. We believe that Jesus died and rose again and so we believe that God will bring with Jesus those who have fallen asleep in him. According to the Lord's own word, we tell you that we who are still

HIS INSTRUCTIONS ON PREACHING

> alive, who are left till the coming of the Lord, will certainly not precede those who have fallen asleep. For the Lord himself will come down from heaven, with a loud command, with the voice of the archangel and with the trumpet call of God, and the dead in Christ will rise first. After that, we who are still alive and are left will be caught up together with them in the clouds to meet the Lord in the air. And so we will be with the Lord forever. Therefore encourage each other with these words (1 Thessalonians 4:13-18).

This was a message of hope as he preached on the resurrection of Christ and the cross, which was central to his messages, as seen in those recorded in the book of Acts.

In his second letter, he wrote to correct some misunderstandings regarding the Lord's second coming. Furthermore, he thanked God for them, whom the Lord loved, and urged them to stand firm and hold fast to the truth, writing:

> But we ought always to thank God for you, brothers loved by the Lord, because from the beginning God chose you to be saved through the sanctifying work of the Spirit and through belief in the truth. He called you to this through the gospel, that you might share in the glory of our Lord Jesus Christ. So then, brothers, stand firm and hold to the teachings we passed on to you, whether by word of mouth or by letter (2 Thessalonians 2:13-15).

So whether by preaching or letter, he prayed and worked to encourage and strengthen the Thessalonians and others in every good deed and word. He asked them to pray for him and his fellow workers that the message of the Lord may have full course and spread rapidly and be honored just as it had been with them (2 Thessalonians 2:16-3:1).

Timothy and Titus

In the pastoral letters, Paul used the many expressions that proclaim the word of God previously mentioned above. In his first letter to Timothy, he warned the young the minister about false teachers of the law and gave instructions regarding the church and its leaders. He reminded Timothy of his own calling, writing, "I was appointed a herald and an apostle ... and a teacher of the true faith to the Gentiles" (1 Timothy 2:7). And he made this appeal:

> I urge, then, first of all, that requests, prayers, intercession and thanksgiving be made for everyone—for kings and all those in authority, that we may live peaceful and quiet lives, in all godliness and holiness. This is good, and pleases God our Savior, who wants all men to be saved and come to a knowledge of the truth. For there is one God and one mediator between God and men, the man Christ Jesus, who gave himself as a ransom for all men—the testimony given in its proper time (1 Timothy 2:1-6).

Thus, Paul gave this appeal to Timothy, worthy of acceptance, writing:

> This is a trustworthy saying that deserves full acceptance (and for this we labor and strive), that we have put our hope in the living God, who is the Savior of all men, and especially those who believe. Command and teach these things. Don't let anyone look down on you because you are young, but set an example for the believers in speech, in life, in love, in faith and in purity. Until I come, devote yourself to the public reading of Scripture, to preaching and to teaching. Do not neglect your gift, which was given you through a prophetic message when the body of elders laid hands on you (1 Timothy 4:9-14).

He was to be diligent in these matters and to give himself wholly to them so that everyone might see his progress. If he would do these things, he would assure the salvation of many of his hearers (1 Timothy 4:15-16).

To ministers and leaders of the church, he wrote to Timothy the following important matters:

> The elders who direct the affairs of the church well are worthy of double honor, especially those whose work is preaching and teaching. For the Scripture says, 'Do not muzzle the ox while it is treading out the grain,' and 'The worker deserves his wages.' Do not entertain an accusation against an elder unless it is brought by two or three witnesses. Those who sin are to be rebuked publicly, so that the others may take warning (1 Timothy 5:17-20).

In this passage Paul declares an Old Testament passage Deuteronomy 25:4 and a New Testament passage Luke 10:7, both as Scripture.

Furthermore, he warned against the love of money, a root of all kinds of evil, for some have wandered from the faith and pierced themselves with grief trying to get rich and fall into ruin (1 Timothy 6:6-10). Then he closed the letter with this admonition, writing:

> Timothy, guard what has been entrusted to your care. Turn away from godless chatter and the opposing ideas of what is falsely called knowledge, which some have professed and in so doing have wandered from the faith (1 Timothy 6:20-21).

In his second letter to Timothy, his last letter and his swan song, Paul reminded him once again of his calling to be a herald, an apostle, and a teacher. He gave this admonition for diligence and faithfulness in service:

> For this reason I remind you to fan into flame the gift of God, which is in you through the laying on of my hands. For God did not give us a spirit of timidity, but a spirit of power, of love, and of self-discipline. So do not be ashamed to testify about our Lord, or ashamed of me his prisoner. But join with me in suffering for the gospel, by the power of God, who has saved us and called us to a holy life—not because of anything we have done but because of his own purpose and grace. This grace was given us in Christ Jesus before the beginning of time, but it has now been revealed through the appearing of our Savior, Christ

HIS INSTRUCTIONS ON PREACHING

Jesus, who has destroyed death and has brought life and immortality to light through the gospel (2 Timothy 1:6-10).

He appealed to Timothy to be strong in the grace that is in Christ. He was to entrust the things that Paul taught him to reliable men who would be qualified to teach others. Furthermore, he needed to endure hardship like a good soldier of Christ (2 Timothy 2:1-3).

Moreover, he was to keep reminding these men of the following matters:

> Warn them before God against quarreling about words; it is of no value, and only ruins those who listen. Do your best to present yourself to God as one approved, a workman who does not need to be ashamed and who correctly handles the word of truth. Avoid godless chatter, because those who indulge in it will become more and more ungodly (2 Timothy 2:14-16).

In addition, he was to flee youthful lusts and pursue righteousness, faith, love, and peace along with all those who call on the Lord out of a pure heart (2 Timothy 2:22).

Paul reminded Timothy about his teaching, his way of life, and his purpose, even during persecutions and sufferings. He also warned him about evil men and imposters (2 Timothy 3:1-13). But Timothy was urged to continue in his ministry in the following ways:

> But as for you, continue in what you have learned and have become convinced of because you know those from whom you learned it, and how from infancy you have known the holy Scriptures, which are able to make you wise for salvation through faith in Christ Jesus. All Scripture is God-breathed and is useful for teaching, rebuking, correcting and training in righteousness, so that the man of God may be thoroughly equipped for every good work (2 Timothy 3:14-17).

The key to his ministry was the holy Scriptures which would equip him for every work that he was called to do.

Then he charged him in the presence of God to preach the word of God and to do the work on an evangelist in the following ways:

> In the presence of God and of Christ Jesus, who will judge the living and the dead, and in view of his appearing and his kingdom, I give you this charge: Preach the Word; be prepared in season and out of season; correct, rebuke and encourage—with great patience and careful instruction. For the time will come when men will not put up with sound doctrine. Instead, to suit their own desires, they will gather around them a great number of teachers to say what their itching ears want to hear. They will turn their ears away from the truth and turn aside to myths. But you, keep your head in all situations, endure hardship, do the work of an evangelist, discharge all the duties of your ministry (2 Timothy 4:1-5).

Paul knew that his ministry in this world was concluding and his departure was coming soon, but he had the following consolation:

> For I am already being poured out like a drink offering, and the time has come for my departure. I have fought the good fight, I have finished the race, I have kept the faith. Now there is in store for me the crown of righteousness, which the Lord, the righteous Judge, will award me on that day—and not only to me, but also to all who have longed for his appearing (2 Timothy 4:6-8).

In his defense before Roman rulers, no one came to stand with him, but he graciously hoped that this would not be held against them. But he was assured of this:

> But the Lord stood at my side and gave me strength, so that through me the message might be fully proclaimed and all the Gentiles might hear it. And I was delivered from the lion's mouth. The Lord will rescue me from every evil attack and bring me safely to his heavenly kingdom. To him be glory for ever and ever. Amen (2 Timothy 4:17-18).

To Titus, Paul wrote and reminded this fellow minister that he was a servant of God and an apostle of Jesus Christ, as he had mentioned in other letters. At the promised time, he brought to light the word of God through the proclamation of the gospel that was entrusted to him by the command of God our Savior (Titus 1:1-3).

He gave Titus the qualifications of an elder, which would include pastors, preachers, evangelists, and other ministers, who should be able to teach, just as he wrote in his first letter to Timothy (1 Timothy 3:1-7). These persons should have the following qualities:

> An elder must be blameless, the husband of but one wife, a man whose children believe and are not open to the charge of being wild and disobedient. Since an overseer is entrusted with God's work, he must be blameless—not overbearing, not quick-tempered, not given to drunkenness, not violent, not pursing dishonest gain. Rather he must be hospitable, one who loves what is good, who is self-controlled, upright, holy and disciplined. He must hold firmly to the trustworthy message as it has been taught, so that he can encourage others by sound doctrine and refute those who oppose it (Titus 1:6-9).

In this passage Paul emphasized in closing to hold fast to the trustworthy message so that he could encourage other believers by sound doctrine and refute those who oppose the faithful word of God. He was to rebuke sharply these rebellious people, mere talkers and deceivers, with all authority and not let anyone despise him. The things written in this letter must be taught (Titus 2:15-3:1-7).

He closed his instructions in this letter to Titus about people who were foolish, disobedient, and enslaved by all kinds of passions and lusts before salvation, writing:

> But when the kindness and love of God our Savior appeared, he saved us, not

because of righteous things we have done, but because of his mercy. He saved us through the washing of rebirth and renewal by the Holy Spirit, whom he poured out on us generously through Jesus Christ our Savior, so that, having been justified by his grace, we might become heirs having the hope of eternal life. This is a trustworthy saying. And I want you to stress these things, so that those who have trusted in God may be careful to devout themselves to doing what is good. These things are excellent and profitable for everyone (Titus 3:4-8).

These pastoral letters, like most of Paul's letters, emphasized the need of faithful leaders to stand fast in the faith, to proclaim the word of God, and to watch for deceitful men who distort the truth and who lead churches and believers astray. Furthermore, these letters specify the qualifications of leaders, and they should emphasize the trustworthy message of Christ as Savior and Lord, which they should teach and preach.

SUMMARY

Many Christians would consider the Apostle Paul the prince of preachers. He certainly ranks among the greatest. He refers to preaching first in his calling by God to be a preacher, an apostle, and a teacher.

His Life

In the book of Acts, Paul was first known as Saul of Tarsus, the zealous Jewish Pharisee who was persecuting the early Christians. He met the Lord in a shining light from heaven on the road to Damascus and committed his life to him. He was called to take the message of salvation in Christ to the Gentiles, called to be a preacher, an apostle, and a teacher of the word of God. He was accepted reluctantly at first by the apostles and disciples, but after several years of study in Arabia and in ministry in Tarsus, he was commissioned to take the gospel to Asia Minor and on into Europe on four missionary journeys, preaching the gospel of Jesus Christ, establishing churches throughout the known world, ordaining ministers to lead them, and writing thirteen letters that became Scripture, developing and clarifying the truths of the word of God.

Paul was first of all a preacher of the gospel among his several callings, preaching the word of God in the power of the Spirit and deep conviction in winning multitudes to Christ and training them in the Lord's work. This came through preaching, teaching, and writing, including much about the proclamation of the word of God by example and through his letters. He suffered much in his life through opposition to the gospel through the Jews and persecution, including imprisonment. He was able to establish the foundational truth that people are saved by grace through faith in Jesus Christ, not by works, through the proclamation and defense of the gospel, as recorded in the book of Acts. After thirty-five years of ministry and having fought the good fight of faith, he left a legacy of life and service. His conversion to Christ and his testimony to Jews and Gentiles recorded in Scripture are critical statements because the gospel of Christ is for everyone and must be received by faith in him in order to receive salvation.

His Character

Saul of Tarsus was a Jew of the dispersion with a strong religious and moral character, but was dogmatic and misguided leading to persecution of the church. He was influenced by Greek and Roman culture. After his conversion by Christ, his love for the Lord was his dominating characteristic and his motivation for service. He dedicated his life wholeheartedly to the Lord early in life after a struggle with sin. The Spirit of God gave him the victory, preparing him for his great world mission.

He was determined to fulfill his calling of proclaiming the gospel, especially to the Gentiles, which he kept and fulfilled to the end of his life. By the power of the Holy Spirit who filled his new life from the very beginning, he preached fearlessly with great boldness, confounding his critics. He won many to Christ and motivated them to service, though with resistance, suffering, and persecution by enemies.

After he was saved, his views of righteousness were completely changed from the righteousness of the Jewish law to the righteousness of God through the gospel. He realized that the righteous ones live by faith, not by works. Thus, Paul preached that people are saved by grace through their personal faith in Christ accomplished through the cross and the resurrection. Though he always began by taking the gospel first to the Jews, his ultimate commitment and concern was to take the gospel to the Gentiles throughout the Roman world. He was a man of prayer from the beginning to the end of his ministry, praying, praising, interceding, and thanking God on behalf of the Jews and all men that they might be saved through faith in Christ and confess him as Lord. He was solely dependent upon the guidance and direction of the Lord throughout his world mission of proclaiming the gospel through patience in many trials, sufferings, and persecutions, but with effectiveness in winning many to Christ and to service for him.

His Messages

The recorded messages of Paul are provided in the book of Acts. They were written by Luke as inspired by the Holy Spirit. The first was delivered to the Jews primarily in Antioch of Pisidia in which he provided a survey of God's work with the people of Israel from Moses to John the Baptist. Paul concluded with a presentation of the gospel of Jesus' suffering unto death but rising from the dead as prophesied. He appealed for faith in Christ for the forgiveness of sins and everything that the law of Moses could not do. In Athens when he saw the idolatry of the Gentiles, he disputed with the Epicureans and Stoics, and at the Areopagus proclaimed Jesus and the resurrection which they thought were some new gods. He explained to them that the true God who gives life and breath to everyone is not to be liken to idols, but calls on men to repent and believe in Christ. God will judge the world by him whom he appointed since he raised him from the dead. In Miletus he delivered a pastoral message to the Ephesian elders reminding them of his example of faithful service urging them to be good shepherds of God's flock. He warned them that men would come and scatter the church of God. He concluded by reminding them to help the poor and of Jesus' word that it is more blessed to give than receive.

In his last recorded messages, Paul gave his testimony and offered a defense of the faith. In Jerusalem he presented his testimony of his past life and his conversion, and his call to take the gospel to the Gentiles. His audience was a hostile crowd who reacted violently, wanting to kill him. He was rescued by the Romans and sent to Caesarea. Here he again defended the faith stressing the resurrection of the dead, which the Jewish leaders rejected, but the Gentiles wanted to hear more about the matter. Later the Roman governor allowed him to defend himself in the presence of King Agrippa and both Jewish and Gentile leaders. The Jews, in response to his

SUMMARY 75

claims, remained hostile, but the Gentiles concluded that he was not guilty of the charges, but sent him to Rome to appear before Caesar since he made an appeal as a Roman citizen. Luke ended in the book of Acts with his ministry there.

His Doctrine

The doctrines prominent in Paul's messages in Acts are concentrated on the person of Christ, the gospel, and the way of salvation. From the beginning he preached that Jesus is the Son of God, the Jewish Messiah, the Christ, since at first his audiences were primarily Jews. But he proclaimed the gospel throughout his ministry emphasizing that Christ must suffer unto death for the sins of people according to the prophets such as Isaiah. Furthermore, he rose again according to the Scriptures as predicted in the Psalms. The resurrection was the proof that God was satisfied with Christ's payment for sin and that he is truly the Son of the living God with power to save those who would trust in him. All the recorded messages stressed this great truth except the pastoral message to the Ephesian elders at Miletus.

Furthermore, salvation from sin and its consequences must be received by faith in Christ. The believer is justified by faith from all things that the law of Moses could not accomplish, nor works that anyone can do. Salvation is provided and offered to Jews and Gentiles by grace, and Gentiles do not need to keep the ceremonial laws to be saved. The first church council in Jerusalem resolved this conflict. When Paul preached to a predominantly Jewish audience, he surveyed the history of Israel showing how God had worked in history to prepare a people to work out his plan of salvation. He described how God predicted the coming of the Messiah fulfilling prophecy. Many of the Jews accepted him as Savior and Lord, but others rejected him, especially the Jewish leaders who persecuted the Christians. However the gospel was taken to the Gentiles, and great numbers were saved and became members and leaders of the church. These were counseled by Paul through his example, instruction, and encouragement to the Ephesian elders. Many other doctrines and instructions are described in Paul's letters to the churches and leaders.

His Organization

Paul's recorded messages do not give many details as to how he organized his messages, but does give some general principles. These recorded messages inspired by the Spirit indicate that they are topical messages drawn from his purpose in the light of the need of his audience. They are introduced in a brief manner based on the occasion, the need, the direction of the Spirit of God, and the revelation of Old Testament Scripture.

The subjects are developed around two or three main points. Luke recorded these messages from reports of eye witnesses, from his observations when he was present to hear them, and from Paul himself who delivered the messages. They are centered around his personal experience of salvation and his exposition of the gospel of Christ, namely, his death on the cross for man's forgiveness of sin, and especially the resurrection of Christ, the proof that he is the Son of God with power to save. They were focused on the audience: Jews, Gentiles, or the people of God.

Paul concluded his messages with an appeal to the hearts and lives of the persons in the audience. This appeal was for them to accept God's offer of salvation and service for Christ and a warning not to reject the offer as the prophets said would happen to many. He appealed to unbelievers to trust in Christ for forgiveness of sins based on the gospel and for believers to continue in the faith and in service for the Lord. Many of the Jews, especially the leaders, rejected his appeals and became antagonistic; so Paul turned to the Gentiles more and more as they received Christ and the gospel.

His Style

Style of the Christian speaker depends on his physical, mental, psychological, and especially his spiritual qualities. This includes clarity, force, elegance, and imagination combined in a way that he develops his message and delivers it to is audience. Paul did not have impressive physical gifts, but he did have physical endurance and mental capacity, trained under the tutelage of Gamaliel. He could speak and write in the *koine* Greek, the predominate language of the Roman empire, and also in Aramaic, the colloquial language of Palestine. He was strong-willed and dogmatic, which were an asset after he had been converted to Christ. His spiritual qualities and gifts were far superior to his other abilities. He was filled with the Spirit, and his love of God was manifested in his life and ministry. He was called to be a preacher, an apostle, and a teacher of the Gentiles. He was assisted by gifted preachers and disciples and depended on the inspired Scriptures that equipped him for every good work, especially preaching the word of God in all seasons.

Paul spoke in the language of the people with clarity, preaching the word of God fearlessly. His audiences understood his message, and though many accepted Christ and followed him, others rejected his message, which they understood plainly, because of jealousy and hardness of heart. He began where the people were in understanding and sought to lead them to accept the claims of Christ. His clarity of thought contributed to his forcefulness of expression. He had an ability to adapt to audiences of various sizes and religious understanding. He took advantage of unique occasions and opportunities to gain the attention of the people. He spoke the word of God not only with words but also with the power of the Holy Spirit, with much assurance, and with an acceptable manner of life before the Lord.

His Power and Effectiveness

Shortly after his conversion, Paul was commissioned to take the name of Christ to the Gentiles. He was filled with the Holy Spirit and power and spoke boldly and

SUMMARY 77

with effectiveness to reach Jews and Gentiles with the gospel. He grew more and more powerful and won many Jews to Christ, but was rejected by their leaders. He eventually was accepted by the apostles, and after several years of study and preparation, he was sent with Barnabas to spread the word of God to Asia Minor. He went to the Jews first in these areas, and many of them and proselytes in the synagogues accepted the good news of Christ, but many would not believe and stirred up opposition with persecution. However, they established many churches with Jewish disciples and many Gentiles who received the word of God gladly. On his second missionary journey, he entered the Greek world by the direction of the Spirit and was effective in reaching more and more Gentiles.

At Athens the Greek philosophers were skeptical but interested in hearing about Jesus and the resurrection. In this idolatrous city with an altar TO AN UNKNOWN GOD, the people were introduced to the known God by Paul, when given the opportunity to speak at the Aeropagus. The response to his message was minimal, but the seeds of the word of God were sown, and in years later the church there grew and prospered. On his third missionary journey he was successful in the strategic city of Ephesus and the surrounding areas, winning many Gentiles to Christ, establishing churches, encouraging leaders, and establishing a center for evangelism and church growth. Finally, he returned to Jerusalem where the church leaders wholeheartedly agreed that the Lord had opened the door to the Gentiles without restrictions. Here he gave his testimony, and when he explained that he was commissioned to take the gospel to the Gentiles, the Jews sought to kill him. At Caesarea he presented his testimony, and though declared innocent, he was sent to Rome to appear before Caesar's court. He was well received by the believers and allowed to live in a rented house under guard, but he reached many more for Christ who came to hear him. He continued to preach boldly the kingdom of God without interference and taught concerning the Lord Jesus Christ.

During his more than thirty-five years of ministry, he took the gospel to the Jews first, but eventually he turned to preach to the Gentiles and won many to Christ in the known Roman world, established churches, ordained ministers, defended the faith, and wrote letters to leaders, many of which were preserved for us as inspired Scriptures. He serves as an example to ministers and churches in dedication, in ministry, in evangelizing the world, and in church growth.

His Instructions on Preaching

Paul wrote extensively about many matters in his letters, and especially about preaching, using seven different expressions, particularly the words preaching (*kerygma*) and preaching the gospel (*euangelizesthai*). In his letter to the Romans, his emphasis was on the content of preaching based on the gospel and the scope of preaching, particularly to the Gentiles. In his Corinthian letters he stressed the preaching of the gospel, not with words of human wisdom, but with the wisdom and power of God through the message of the cross and the resurrection of Christ. The preachers were called by God and gifted by the Spirit of God for the task.

In the letter to the Galatians, he was especially concerned about men who were preaching another gospel, that is, perverting the gospel by requiring the Gentiles to keep the customs of the Jewish laws. To the Ephesians he declared that the holy apostles and prophets revealed the mystery of Christ in which the Gentiles were to be fellow heirs with the Jews in the gospel of salvation. Gifted leaders prepared God's people for service in building the body of Christ, the church. In his letter to the Philippians, he emphasized that preachers should preach the word of God courageously and fearlessly in defense of the gospel. In that day even many in Caesar's household received Christ, but warned about those who preached out of envy and rivalry. To the Colossians he addressed the similar problems of the prison letters to the Ephesians and the Philippians, such as the proclamation of the mystery of Christ that God made known that the gospel was for the Gentiles also. He requested prayer that doors of opportunity would open to preach with power and effectiveness.

In his letters to the Thessalonians, Paul emphasized the need to preach the gospel, not only with words but also with power, with the Holy Spirit, and with deep conviction. But also he urged them to preach in spite of opposition of evil men and in hope of the second coming of Christ, encouraging believers to remain steadfast in service for him.

In his pastoral letters he reminded Timothy and Titus to remain faithful in their service, give instructions to the churches, and state the qualifications for ministers, warning them of false teachers who distort the truth and lead Christians astray. He encouraged them to be strong in the faith and preach the word of God in all seasons. He reminded them that all Scripture is inspired by God and profitable to equip them for every good work, including doing the work of an evangelist. He warned against the love of money that leads to a departure from the faith and to ruin and grief. He closed his second letter to Timothy, in the light of his departure from this life, that he had fought the good fight, he had finished the race, and he had kept the faith.

CONCLUSION

The Apostle Paul is Prince of Preachers, exemplified in the book of Acts and in his New Testament letters. His ministry began with his conversion to Christ on the road to Damascus when the Lord confronted him, and he responded by faith that saved him by God's grace. He was called to be the apostle to the Gentiles and empowered by the Spirit for service. Over the years he manifested the true character of a minister through his love for Christ, his dedication in service, his determination to fulfill his calling, his boldness in the proclamation of the gospel, his righteous living, his faith in the Lord, his vision in missions, and his prayerfulness in ministry.

His recorded messages in the book of Acts are representative discourses of his ministry inspired by the Spirit. He appealed to the Jews first through the work of God in the Old Testament era and through the fulfillment of prophecies by Jesus, through the gospel in his death, burial, and resurrection for the sins of mankind. He proclaimed that the Gentiles were included in God's plan of salvation, who are received through faith without having to keep the customs of the Jewish laws. His doctrines were focused on Jesus Christ as the Son of God; the gospel of Christ who was crucified for the sins of men and resurrected for their justification; salvation by grace through faith to all who will come to him; the work of God in history; and pastoral care of Christians through his ministers.

Paul's messages are topical in nature based on the needs of the people and on their background and understanding. His content includes Old Testament Scripture and background, his personal experiences with Christ, and the truths of the gospel, especially the cross and the resurrection, which is the ultimate proof of his deity and his power to save man. His style in preaching was to speak in the language of the people with clarity and simplicity and with boldness and forcefulness in the power of the Holy Spirit.

He preached the word of God, not in words alone but also in power, in the Holy Spirit, and in much assurance. He was filled with the Spirit and preached fearlessly under persecution, to the Jews first and then to the Gentiles, his primary mission. He was effective in winning many Jews and Gentiles to Christ in much of the Roman world, establishing churches, ordaining ministers, defending the Christian faith in the midst of great opposition, and writing thirteen letters which are preserved as inspired Scripture.

In his letters he emphasized the gospel of Christ in his death for our sins and his resurrection which declared him to be the Son of God with power to save mankind. Christ is proclaimed as Savior by grace through faith, not of works, including works of the law proposed by the enemies of God, which he declared was false doctrine. Christians are empowered by God's indwelling Spirit to live uprightly and to do what is pleasing to him. Ministers are empowered to proclaim the cross in the wisdom and power of God, not men, in order to persuade people to trust Christ and serve him. Ministers are instructed to live holy lives, to dedicate themselves in service for Christ, to set examples for the churches and Christians, to lead them in serving the Lord, and to warn them against evil men and false doctrine. He defended the faith and contended for the faith, which is the whole body of Christian truth.

The apostle Paul is truly the model for ministers and churches in proclaiming the gospel to the world and fulfilling the great commission. He accomplished this by his commitment to Christ, his call to be a minister, his love for the Lord, his decisive dedication to serve him, his power and boldness to proclaim the gospel to the world and establish churches, and to lead ministers and churches to fulfill their ministry for Christ. All ministers and Christians must decide by God's direction and power how they will serve the Lord.

"Be filled with the Spirit," wrote the Apostle Paul (Ephesians 5:18b).

REFERENCES

Adams, Jay E., *Audience Adaptations in the Sermons and Speeches of Paul*. Grand Rapids, MI: Baker Book House, 1956.

Bailey, Raymond, *Paul the Preacher*. Nashville: Broadman Press, 1991, helpful in analyzing Paul's rhetoric and adaptation of his message to the world.

Beaudean, John, *Paul's Theology of Preaching,* Dissertation Series, no. 6. Macon, GA: Mercer University Press, 1988.

Chamberlain, Charles Abiel, "The Preaching of the Apostle Paul, Based on a Study of the Acts of the Apostles and Paul's Letters, with Special Reference to the First and Second Corinthians." S.T.D., Temple University School of Theology, 1959.

Eadie, John, *Paul the Preacher*. New York: Robert Carter and Brothers, 1860, practical exposition of Paul's speeches.

Gericke, Paul W., "Great Preachers of the Church." Manuscript, 2000, a survey of the outstanding preachers of the church from the Lord Jesus Christ and the Apostle Paul to Evangelist Billy Graham.

Murphy-O'Connor, Jerome, *Paul on Preaching*. New York: Sheed and Ward, 1964, a discussion of the place of preaching in the Catholic Church in the light of the teachings of Paul.

Sunukjian, Donald, "Patterns for Preaching: a Rhetorical Analysis of the Sermons of Paul in Acts 13, 17, and 20." Th.D., Dallas Theological Seminary, 1972.

Swindoll, Charles R., *Paul: A Man of Grace and Grit*. Nashville: W Publishing Group, 2002, a popular biography.

BIOGRAPHICAL SKETCH

Dr. Gericke was born in 1924 and raised in St. Louis, Missouri. He served in the U.S. Navy Air Corps from 1942-46 in the field of radio, radar, and loran. He received the Bachelor of Science degree in Electrical Engineering from Washington University, St. Louis, in 1949, and served for a time in teaching electronics.

When he became a Christian in 1951, he believed the Lord had called him into the ministry. He was licensed and ordained to the ministry in the Southern Baptist Convention. While he continued his education for the ministry, he served churches in Missouri, Kentucky, and Mississippi. During this time, he studied for the ministry at the Southern Baptist Theological Seminary in Louisville, Kentucky, receiving the Bachelor of Divinity degree in 1960; at the New Orleans Baptist Theological Seminary, receiving the Doctor of Theology degree in 1964; and at the University of New Orleans, receiving the Master of Education degree in 1972.

He served on the staff and faculty of the New Orleans Baptist Theological Seminary from 1961 to 1993, serving in various capacities, particularly Director of the Library and professor teaching homiletics and communications. He led in the founding and the development of radio station WBSN-FM on campus and the communication center for training students in the use of radio and television to proclaim the gospel of Jesus Christ to all the world. He is the author of five other books: *The Preaching of Robert G. Lee*, *The Ministers Filing System*, *Sermon Building*, *Crucial Experiences in the Life of D. L. Moody*, and *Pastor's Library*. After his retirement from the faculty in 1993, he served another six years on the staff of the North Georgia Campus of the Seminary in the Metro Atlanta area, retiring in 1999.

www.ingramcontent.com/pod-product-compliance
Lightning Source LLC
Chambersburg PA
CBHW021835300426
44114CB00009BA/449